The Daily Lion

400 Meditations on Success, Mindset and the Art of Being a Lion

by,

Become the Lion

Book Testimonials

"Your life is nothing but a reflection of your thoughts. Become The Lion's book contains 400 powerful thoughts and quotes that can transform your life. Buy this book today. Read it, live it, and become the lion you were always meant to be."

- Dan Lok,
The King of High-Ticket Sales,
International Best-Selling Author & 2 Times TEDx Speaker

"The Daily Lion is my go-to source for motivation and inspiration. Reading just one passage from this book as a part of your morning routine will prime you and put you in the right mindset to crush your day!"

- Michael Carbone
Founder of michaelcarbone.ca

"It's funny how just a few words strung together can motivate you to take on the world. I basically live my entire life by memes and quotes. This book is full of the best quotes ever quoted (you can quote that)"

- Ryan Stewman
Founder of hardcorecloser.com

"Who you become on your journey is far more important than what you achieve and The Daily Lion is a book that will inspire you on your journey to achieving your dreams"

- David Osborn
Author of Wealth Can't Wait

Acknowledgements:

Before you start reading this book, we want to say thank you for believing in our mission enough to purchase this book. It's been quite an exhilarating journey since starting Become the Lion and it wouldn't have been possible without your help. Without you, we would not be where we are today. Become the Lion has ventured much farther than being just an Instagram page. It is now an international brand that seeks to inspire as many Lions and cubs as possible.

We would like to say thank you to all the Lions out there who have supported us in our journey. Without you and your constant feedback, we never would be where we are today. Through talking with many of you and seeing your comments every day, we feel that we have found our mission in life. And you gave us that.

We would also like to thank our friends and family for believing in our dream as much as we do. It isn't easy believing in someone's dream when they do not make any money from it yet, but our families have stood by us and we will always remember.

Lastly, to the readers of this book. We thank you for taking a chance and buying this book. You are that rare Lion that goes above and beyond. A Lion that takes action and not one who simply glosses over information.

Introduction

This book is meant to inspire you to take charge in your life. To create your own path while developing a strong conviction that you are destined for greatness and that no one can deter you from working towards your ultimate vision.

We were told the same lie that's told to everyone: go to school, get a job and play it safe. We longed for more than a minimal existence. We want to change the world, to leave it a better place after we are gone. This book is a collection of our top 400 quotes we've used since starting our brand that has since inspired millions.

While writing over a 1000 quotes, it was no easy task in cutting it down to 400. We hope we didn't disappointment you in any way. Each quote is flushed with a story or thought depicted from our own lives. You can read one each day or read them all at once, the choice is yours.

But our goal here is not for you to just passively read each quote. Our goal is two-fold, one is while reading this book, you will develop a Lion-like mindset. Our second goal is that you take action. Reading without implementing is not what this book is about. This book is about taking action. So please, read this book slowly, highlight, underline and takes ample notes. Seek to understand each quote and our meaning of it with solid comprehension.

Through this book, realize we started off just like most of you. We were middle-classed raised and from a small town of 6,000 people. We didn't have any connections or an idea on how to start to a business. It was through a vision of ourselves and years of hard work that have produced the men we are today.

Take each quote wholeheartedly and understand that we're here for you each step of your journey. And we know that being a Lion is a lonely road, especially at the beginning. But that doesn't mean you need to be alone. We are here for you and so are your fellow Lions.

We all want to see you succeed and live your ultimate vision.

If you have any questions or are in need of answers do not hesitate to reach out to us: nicholas@becomethelion.com and trevor@becomethelion.com

Take the quotes from the book and use them as a guide for inspiration in your life. And until we talk again, don't stop grinding!

Sincerely,

Nicholas Xifaras and Trevor Oldham

1. **Our degree of greatness isn't defined at birth, it's defined at death** ~ It doesn't matter if you are born poor, in a third-world country, rich, or in a place of power. Why? Because you did not do anything to contribute to it. The only thing that is under your control is what you do while you live. Every waking moment of your day, you are consciously or unconsciously working on your future. And your future will be determined by the work you get done today, not next week or next year. You need to be living in the present but with the foresight that what you do every day will be your future, your legacy. You need to know that the moment you die, you will leave your life's work behind. And then what will you be remembered for? For nothing? For greatness? It's up to you. Wake up each day with a purpose and goals, while getting sh*t done.

2. **I won't stop until I'm at the top ~** This is what Become the Lion is all about... becoming the TOP in your industry while becoming the strongest version of yourself. You have goals that far surpass those of the common. Your aim is to be the TOP in your industry, not region-wide, not country-wide... but the absolute top. You are willing to put in the work required and then more. You do not b*tch or complain. You do not seek to 'fit in' because you realize you have ONE LIFE, and you are going to live that life in the way of the Lion.

3. **Looking back a year from today, I won't even recognize myself. I am going to become the legend I was born to be. ~** Make a pact to yourself that in a year from now, you will not even recognize the person you are today. It's time to burn the boats. Wherever you are at: mediocre, average, great or legendary, aim for higher. Lose all of your bad habits and time wasting activities and loser friends. Absolutely stop everything that is pulling you away from your highest potential... And then start implementing the habits of a legend every damn day. Be the person you were born to be, and that person is one who will achieve greatness. Start today. You have one year.

4. **A reader lives a thousand lives before he dies. The man who never reads lives only one ~** If you are feeling lost, a lack of ideas, a lack of purpose... pick up a damn book. Books are powerful. Books allow you to live vicariously through others, to experience their ups and downs, trials, and successes... all from the comfort of your mind. Too many of us 'can't find time to read' or 'don't like reading'... these are poor excuses. If you want to reach the top, you NEED to be reading at least two books a month... and not just any books, the best books... biographies, histories, success and mindset books. Not bullsh*t novels you read on vacation. The time is now. Get serious with your life and replace all your sheep habits with reading.

5. **Every day I wake up in beast mode ~** If you are not financially free or if you are not living the life you've always dreamed of, there are NO days off.... Period. Going after the 'balance' of life is good ONLY after you are financially free. Every day, when you wake up, you must Become the Lion you were born to be...You must wake up with a beast-like attitude that says 'I will accomplish ALL of my goals for today and let NOTHING get in my way'... this is the way of champions... this is the way of legends. The ones truly at the top don't give a **** about 'excuses' or 'circumstances'. They only care about results... and YOU are the only one that can determine your results, so go all in.

6. **I don't chase dreams. I hunt goals. ~** Everyone has dreams... dreams of a better life, places they want to go, incomes they want to make, and visions they want to ultimately live; but, for most people, they are nothing more than that, just DREAMS. If you ever want to escape that paradigm of just dreaming, it's time to set goals and then work like hell towards accomplishing them. If you are not setting goals, you will NEVER reach your fullest potential. Right now, take some time to write out your top five-year goals and then break them down into yearly, monthly, weekly, and daily milestones. Accomplish all of them and keep yourself accountable during the process. This is how legends are made, so STOP dreaming and START putting in the work towards hunting your goals.

7. **All of us have masterpieces inside of us, the question is, are you willing to write it? ~** Out of all the species you were born human... and humans are powerful beyond measure. Humans have taken over the known world. Humans are the pinnacle of life here on Earth... so don't squander this opportunity by playing life small. You were born for Greatness. Each one of us has a different genetic code that will NEVER be repeated again. It's time you use that uniqueness and become that Great individual you are destined to be. No more games. Create a huge vision for yourself... and then work your vision. Plan, work, plan, work, work... and remember, you have one life, make it legendary.

8. **The number 1 reason people fail in life is because they listen to their friends and family ~** It's not our fault. We grow up in a society where there is a norm, and those that deviate from the norm are life's outcasts. We are trained to go to school, get all these degrees, find a high-paying job, have a family, save, etc. Well, NEWSFLASH: It doesn't have to be like that. You can charter your own life's path...envision a life that is unique to YOU and then WORK towards it. Stop going to your friends and family for advice if they are not where you want to end up in life and, instead, find successful individuals for counsel and advice. They know what they are talking about, so have the courage to pave your own path in this life and the courage to not listen to those who might mean good but are not good for you to take advice from.

9. **Never take your eyes off the target ~** Having a vision is not enough. It's only the first step towards greatness... you must have that vision clearly written down and on a board that is VISIBLE so you can look at it EVERY morning when you wake up. This is the power of immersion. If you don't do this, you will often forget about it after a few week's time... which is what a sheep does... while Lions make sure that they are reminded of their end-goal and that they are on a path towards becoming a legend every damn day. They do not become sidetracked by distractions or 'new opportunities' because they are ABSOLUTELY focused on their mission, purpose and goals. Action step: make a vision and goal board and look at it every day.

10. **A mistake repeated more than once is a decision.** ~ How many times have you made the SAME 'mistake' more than once? Chances are a lot... many of us are quick to say that we will not drink that much, stay up that late, hangout with this person or that group again... and yet, when the time comes, our promise to our self is not upheld. This is a characteristic of life's sheep... Lions honor their self-promises... the next time you make a promise to yourself, stick with it, NO MATTER the 'circumstances'... and just know that there is no such thing as multiple mistakes for the same action, for it is a damn choice to make the same mistake again and again... know this. Live by this.

11. **People who are real do not care about being liked. They care about being respected** ~ Lions do not seek attention; sheep do. Sheep love getting attention by any means possible. They will speak loudly, interrupt, start drama, and have an attitude. They do this because they are seriously insecure, while Lions do not give a f*ck about attention. They know that respect is what matters. They work hard every day, keep to themselves, keep their promises, and are always progressing in the world. They don't have the time or the need to get others constant attention. Besides, with respect, comes the RIGHT attention.

12. **Success is not overnight. It takes years of work and dedication** ~ The 21st century is the century of 'get-rich-quick,' 'instant gratification' and 'entitlement.' Not everyone but most of us are losing the grit that our forefathers had in abundance. We want results without having to put the work required. We see these people becoming 'rich overnight,' yet never thinking of what they had to go through to get there...and I'll tell you, it starts with grinding and hustling at the bottom and it's that grinding/hustling work ethic that will make you super rich over your lifetime. But the problem is, people want to be rich NOW and they FORGET that there is a process. Don't forget. Work like hell now and you will have whatever you want in your future.

13. **If you hear people from my past speak of me, keep in mind they are speaking about a person they do not know anymore ~** When you make a genuine DECISION to change your whole life for the better, people start talking. Your old friends will say you have changed. They will say you are different and taking life 'too seriously.' They will sh*t on you and who you have become while telling others about the old you as if you have never changed. Forget them. Forget what they are saying and what they are thinking. You are different now and no longer a f*cking sheep. You are a lion and Lions don't value the sheep's opinion.

14. **Not all hustle is loud. Sometimes hustle is just you, all alone, grinding, while no one hears ~** Most of the people who say they're 'grinding' on social media, are not. Social media today are filled with these get-rich-quick schemes, 'grinders,' people who post daily about 'putting serious hours in,' and that's good, if they are really doing it, but chances are they are NOT. Most of the hardest workers in the world, people who are in the process of and those who have amassed huge empires, have done so in silence. They do not need to post daily about putting in work, they know they are. They do not need external validation. They are life's game-changers and they ENJOY the internal gratification of success. Action step: Be a Lion, focus on yourself and put in the work, don't just talk about the work.

15. **Learn when to be aggressive and when to be patient ~** Many people are led to believe that being 'patient' and 'trusting' the process ALONE will one day reward them with success, while others believe that the key to success is always being the most aggressive person in the room. Neither of these trains of thought is wrong, they are just not totally right. The key to being successful, to reaching the top, while becoming a powerhouse is using both of them together. You should always be patient about your long-term vision. You should not rush it because then you will never get there. You will accustom yourself to instant gratification. You should rush your short-term goals. Be aggressive with them. Go all out and never back down; see how fast you can accomplish them. This is the path toward ultimate success.

16. **Rock bottom has built more champions than privilege ever did ~ For** the most part, growing up rich and with privileges DOES NOT produce a person of grit. The children whose parents have a lot of money are usually spoiled and don't know the value of a dollar. They have a sense of entitlement and elitism towards 'working,' while those brought up the hard way will be working 10 times as hard because they know what the bottom tastes like. So if you weren't born rich, GOOD. You have grit. You have motivation. You have the drive to get the f*ck out from the bottom and you are willing to work longer than the majority. No more feeling self-pity, it's time to be empowered by coming from the bottom, because the top will feel that much better.

17. **The greatest pleasure in life is doing what people say you cannot do** ~ There will be times in your life when someone doubts you. This doubt could come from family and friends. It's not that they even necessarily doubt you; instead, they love you and they're scared that you might get hurt. You must show them; this is your life. There will be outside forces, haters, as we like to call them, who want you to fail. They want to see your demise. Do you know how you get the better of them? By working when they're hating. Prove others wrong while proving yourself right. Stay true to what you're doing and what you believe in.

18. **Surround yourself with people who believe in your dreams** ~ The world is always going to be negative. The media displays the most horrific stories. People will notice a car accident before they notice a lustrous sunset. With negativity swirling in the air, you have to align yourself with those who are positive. You're going to lose friends along the way. They'll laugh at your dreams, with nasty pessimism. Disengage from these people. Social media can be your greatest asset for finding positive like-minded people. Reach out to people you admire. Hire a coach. Do whatever it takes to surround yourself with people who have the same beliefs.

19. **You only live once. Don't look back on your life with regrets and dreams unfulfilled. Look back thinking "I lived a legendary life"** ~ Many people live as though death is not real. They fill their minds and spend their time on nothing. They put everything off until tomorrow. What they don't realize is that it takes a lifetime to achieve greatness. There is no greater reward than reflecting on your life in old age, realizing you fulfilled your potential, brought your dreams into reality, and destroyed your fears. To have that feeling, you need to start being relentless every damn day. There are only so many tomorrows.

20. **If you have a problem with someone, don't tell the world, tell them and finish it with them** ~ Be a real man. Men don't gossip or talk behind someone's back while never confronting the person. When a real man has a problem with someone, the two of them handle it. They don't need everyone knowing because it's their business. Think of the warriors and cowboys of the past, they settled their problems with a fight or duel. Be like them. Don't be like most men today who text, tweet, and talk to everyone but the person they have a problem with.

21. **The loudest person in the room is the weakest person in the room** ~ Notice the heads of families, heads of companies and leaders of private organizations are always quieter than those lower than them. They listen 10x more than they talk. They handle each situation with the wisdom of years of experience and dealing with people. They understand those that talk a lot, often do not strategize what they are going to say. Which can lead to saying something offensive, out-of-place and ignorant. Powerful people think before they speak. They plan out meetings and negotiations before they take place. They are 5 steps ahead. And they already know the other person is the sucker at the deal table. And if you are not presently successful, quiet yourself and be receptive to everything. Learn from others, read books and find mentors. Become respected by speaking less and speaking with power.

22. **Be so good that they can't ignore you** ~ Whatever your industry is, you should always strive for the absolute top. Aiming for anything lower is mediocre and not worth your time. Talking about being on the top is entirely different than actually living it day in and day out. You need to be working as much as possible every day, and then everyone will know you. You will be an icon, a legend and a public figure. That's what being on the top is all about.

23. **Money never sleeps. Wake up early** ~ It's not a secret that successful people wake up early. Losers sleep in because they go to bed late. They lack priorities. Winners get up early because they realize that what they get done in the morning is 3x what they can get done in the same amount of time at night... The morning is the perfect time to spend time alone. You should be by yourself and be working on yourself for the first 2 hours of the day. Write down the night before the number one thing that will propel you towards your vision and do it first thing in the morning. Get sh*t done. And by the time everyone else is up, you are up to date, growing and have gotten a massive amount of work done.

24. **Never announce your next move unless you are actually going to follow through with it** ~ When people tell others they will do something and end up not doing it, they look like fools. To be a person who is respected, admired, and trusted, you need to keep your word. You only announce or make known things you will actually end up accomplishing. Don't just talk to talk. Once you lie or don't follow through publicly, your reputation is tarnished. Your word is your word. If that doesn't mean anything to you, you are not and will never be a Lion.

25. **Don't be afraid of being outnumbered. A Lion walks alone while the sheep flock together** ~ The journey to the top in any industry is hard as hell. There is no way you will reach the top, or even come close, by following what everyone has always done and obeying every single rule. Be prepared to break the rules and walk alone for most of the way. On this journey, you will be against the crowd, the sheep, the common people. They will harass you, call you names and say you are crazy. You weren't born to be another sheep that follows orders and comes and leaves at a certain time each and every day. You are a Lion, a different type of person who doesn't give a sh*t about what 'they' do or what 'they' say. You are doing this for yourself, your family and your empire. Walk alone.

26. **Relentless individual aren't born, they are made by choice** ~ You can't choose what family you're born into, your neighborhood, or your situation. But you can choose what to do with your life after the fact. A person that is relentless learns to be that way by choice. There is no other way to develop it. Stop looking for the secret pill. You can have all the 'privilege' and 'education' you want and still not become successful. Relentlessness comes from within. If you are not already a relentless person, become one. Right now. It's your choice. Promise yourself you will get your goals done every day no matter what bullsh*t 'circumstance' you might face. It's the only way to become one of the greats.

27. **Behind every successful person, there's a lot of unsuccessful years** ~ People see someone who's successful and call them 'lucky.' As if they were blessed with a skill beyond everyone else's capacity. What they don't understand is that no one is born successful. You can have gifted athleticism or knowledge and still turn out to be a failure. These people believe their gifts are going to take them to the promised land. They forget about the person who's pushed themselves and got through failure and hard times. They have that hunger, that willingness to outwork everyone. Eventually their time will shine. Get rid of the notion about instant gratification. Put your nose to the grindstone. Looking back, it will be worth it. Do you think you'll really care how long it took you to become successful?

28. **Failure is not an option for me. Success is all I envision** ~ Are you scared of starting? Scared of what people might think of you? How about failure? If you keep imagining these events over and over, you are going to attract them into your life. Focus on the positive and what you can handle. Events are going to arise in your life that you don't have any control over. These are the stepping stones toward your success. Understand that with every situation you persevere through, you are becoming stronger. You only fail if you give up. A true Lion knows to never fail, you either win or you learn.

29. **All of us are self-made, but only the successful will admit it** ~ It doesn't matter if you start rich, poor, middle class, without a home or without a family, we all choose our own destiny. Be responsible for your life. Sure, some people are born with many privileges, more money, better looks, but it doesn't matter! I challenge you to take a look at your life and take full responsibility for where you are today. Know that you control your future. Your future failures and success alike. Become successful by planning, setting goals and executing. Look back on your life and say 'I made it, I had the best life I could ever imagine, and I did it on my own.'

30. **Sacrifice your time, sweat, and energy today for a better tomorrow** ~ If you understand this concept, great. But if you live this concept day in and day out, you will have riches, both in money and happiness in your future. To attain success, everlasting success, you need to put in the work now. When everyone else is sleeping, partying and fooling around, you're putting in the work. This is true for all ages, but especially if you are younger. Be willing to sacrifice a few years filled with crazy hours. Over time, you will develop something that could not be reached without this type of dedication. Start today. For yourself, your family and your future.

31. **They used to call me crazy. Now they call me looking for a job** ~ When you start out in any endeavor as a means to chase your dreams, people are going to call you crazy. If Henry Ford and Steve Jobs listened to the naysayers, the world wouldn't be as we know it. Put in the work, the hours that no one else is willing to put in. Average people and society as a whole will look down on you. Odds are that you're going to feel different. As if it's wrong to chase after your dreams. When you encounter setbacks, you're going to question yourself. This is all part of the process of living the life you want. The people who laughed at your dreams will be the same people who call you looking for a job.

32. **I'm not obsessed with the money, I'm obsessed with the freedom** ~ Starting a business for the sole purpose of making money will only last so long. You need a purpose that's beyond yourself. That could be helping others, your family, or being able to quit your 9-5 job. Do you think being forced to show up at a specific time is a great life? Work eighty hours doing something you love. Time won't be a concept when you're passionate about a project. When you're passionate, the money will come in. For me, it's been helping as many people as I can. I knew that, by doing this, I'd be able to achieve the freedom I was looking for. The freedom to have a purpose in this world.

33. **They'll doubt you at the bottom. Then they'll look up to you at the top** ~ The worst thing you can do is to doubt someone. Lions have a pent up past, one where they forgive, but never forget. All Lions started as cubs. They might've been weak, but within in a few years, they're king of the jungle. You used to be the partier or the person who didn't go to college. Your old friends and family believe this is still your persona. They don't understand someone can grow and change. Let these people doubt you, if needed, use it for your daily motivation. Because they can't do something, they want to tell you that you can't do something. Once you're at the top, you'll get the respect you deserve.

34. **When you change your thoughts, you change your world** ~ You might have been told that you need to go to school to become successful. A steady job will allow you to live the life you want. Playing it safe is the best way to go. This is what the average mindset will tell you. When you study millionaires long enough, you learn how they think. It's much different than the poor and middle class. They believe in themselves even when they're not entirely sure of what they're doing. The poor and middle class believe having too much money is bad. They don't realize how many more people you can help by having money. Most of us grew up poor or middle class and have ideologies that don't allow us to have financial freedom. When you study those who have what you want, learning their way of thinking and their habits, it's going to change your world.

35. **Poor people watch TV all the time, rich people read all the time** ~ It's a fact. I want you to truly think about how you spend your 'off time.' If you find yourself goofing off, watching TV, or playing games, it's time to man up. Wherever you are in life, it's your responsibility to choose how you spend your time. You have the ability to change. Want to be successful? Start studying successful people. Break down their day-to-day schedules and routine and start implementing their habits into your own life. You need to think success and do as they do before you see success in your own life.

36. **Good men are hard to find because they are usually busy working** ~ This is specifically for the women out there who can't find the 'right guy.' If you are a woman, know that the right guy doesn't have all the free time in the world because he is actually getting sh*t done. They often work longer hours than most, while loving what they do. The only guy who can give you all his time is either broke or close to it. Remember that. You want a gentleman. A man who guides. A leader who isn't a pushover and does everything you want.

37. **The distance between your dreams and reality is called action** ~ We all have dreams. Why do some people accomplish their dreams, while most watch them wither away? Thinking and visualizing your dreams is not enough. You can create a life map for yourself and still not end up at the destination you desired. Your dreams become a reality by taking massive action. You can't work five days and take two days off if you want to be successful. You'll be able to work someone's entire year in four months. The more work you put into yourself, the quicker your dream will happen. You can have the greatest idea in the world but, if you don't put in the work, it'll never come to fruition. Do yourself a favor today and start grinding!

38. **To change your life, change your priorities** ~ To get to where you want to go in life, you can't do what you have always done. Instead of going out and drinking, stay home. You'll awake the next morning, hang-over-free, feeling fresh and ready to conquer the world. If you're not living the life you want, something needs to be done. Write down your day-to-day actions for a week to understand why you aren't successful. When you focus on the future, getting rid of short-term pleasures, your life will start to change.

39. Every person is locked into the world of their own imagination ~ If you think of yourself as one of life's losers, you will be. But if you think of yourself as one of life's winners, chances are you will find more success and opportunities than those of the timid. Your imagination should always be evolving. Any limiting beliefs or self-imposed barriers should be pushed away. Imagination describes the limits of what we can do or become. Besides blind luck, for instance winning the lottery, you can never expand beyond the horizons that are outlined by your mind. If you see yourself as a middle-class earner, and you find it crazy to think yourself as anything else, the odds are almost certain you will not become anything more. Start today by consciously changing your mindset into one of abundance.

40. You need to be ruthless on your way to the top ~ Many people are okay with a normal job, a manager position, a five/six-figure salary. Many love five-day workweeks, paid vacation time, paid sick days, and weekends to do whatever. But the true killers in business and in life can't even think like that, although there is nothing wrong with it. If you want to be at the top of your industry, you must be absolutely ruthless on your way up. You have to lose your loser friends who bring you down, time-wasting activities, 'hobbies' and anything else that will take away from your end result. Make the right connections, do the extra learning, and work outside of the office. Be a killer in your industry, and watch your back during the climb because everyone wants to take it from you!

41. Sometimes you need to walk through fire to get what you want in life ~ Life isn't going to be easy; actually, it's going to be anything but. You're going to have to do things you don't like to do. Friendships fall to ruin, waking up before the sunrise, working weekends, you'll accept these on your journey. Sacrifices will have to be made. It's hard, but every successful person out there has also gone through it. Don't look for sympathy, because it's not easy for any of us. We all have these paradigms that we hold onto for far too long. When you're at your darkest point, remember there's still light shining somewhere. When you face the fire of life, walk out the other side with your hands in triumph.

42. **The most dangerous competitor is not a person, it's a power couple. Choose your partner wisely** ~ Your partner is either going to make you or break you—there's no in-between. This is the person you'll spend the majority of your time around. There are things in your life you simply cannot control; this is not one of them. If you're in a relationship, you can tell if he or she is the right person for you. Lions aren't blinded by love. They know their course and their partner must understand as well. Find someone who's going to push you and make you a better version of yourself. The guy or girl you're looking for won't be at the club come Friday and Saturday. They'll be attending seminars, doing work at coffee shops, or at the gym. Those are a few places you can start. Don't ever stop looking for this person, they're out there. Once you find that person, make sure to never let them go.

43. **Keep your sex life, bank account, and next move private** ~ How many of you go on and on about each of these? Hopefully not many. And if you do, stop. These are the three subjects that people lie and exaggerate about. Know and understand that fully. Real men and women keep their personal business their personal business. They don't feel the need to tell everyone each and every detail of their life. They are confident in what they do and who they are. They can sit back and listen to the fools who let every detail in their life become public.

44. **Read books, have mentors, learn every day, but be you. Your individuality is your power to inspire and rise to greatness** ~ Greatness comes by being authentic. Greatness comes from learning everything in your industry and then creating new ideas and innovations. You can't do that unless you are thinking for yourself and being your own person. The leaders who have amassed a huge following are all individuals, not copies. Think: Muhammad Ali, Arnold Schwarzenegger, Dwayne 'The Rock' Johnson, and Steve Jobs. These people created their own path, but not by following others.

45. **If you're not living your dream, then you're sleeping too much** ~ All over the world, people wake up each day. Most of them hit the snooze button. Do you think you'd be doing that if you were chasing your dreams? Sleep is good when kept to a minimum. I'm talking seven to eight hours of sleep per night. Yet, some people love sleeping ten-plus hours each day. Then, you have to account for the naps they take. You can start to understand why they aren't successful. You should hate sleep because it's taking away from your passion. Be so excited for the next day that it's hard to contain the excitement as you lay there. There's no reason why you should ever be waking up past 8:00 am. Don't you wonder why the successful get up before the rest of the population?

46. **Formal education will make you a living. Self-education will make you a fortune** ~ We're told to go to school. This seems like practical advice if you wish to get ahead in the world. There's only one part that's missing: They don't tell you to keep studying once you get out of high school or college. The average person reads one book per year, the average CEO reads sixty books per year. You can go on YouTube right now and learn from Tony Robbins, Gary Vaynerchuk, Grant Cardone, etc. There has never been a better time to learn information. Learn from the leaders of the world, the ones who have proven results.

47. **If your friends are weighing you down, it's time to leave them and find those that will push you to the next level** ~ It doesn't matter how self-disciplined you may be. If you hang out with losers, those who party, drink, and smoke to excess and waste your time, you will never reach your potential. You may get ahead by yourself, but if you traded those friends and leveled-up and surrounded yourself with those who are reading, working, and planning their future, your own life will grow exponentially. People are infectious; you take from those around you. Starting today, make an analysis of your friends and, if they are not helping, leave them. It's a tough move, but it will be the best decision looking back on your life.

48. **If you're not where you want to be in life, then do something about it** ~ People want to complain about their life situation, but don't want to do anything to change it. You always have the choice on what you want your life to be. You hate your job? Quit. You might say, "I can't quit. I need the money." Do you think that's how true Lions think? Some people choose greatness while others want pity; which one are you? We all have our own problems, but you don't need to share yours with Facebook or the world, keep that private. Unless you're willing to take massive action, you are never going to get anything you want in life. When you decide enough is enough and start to take massive action, the 'lucky' breaks are going to fall your way.

49. **Cocky is loud. Confidence is silent. Know the difference** ~ As they say, 'the loudest person in the room is the weakest person in the room.' Notice that the heads of families, leaders of empires and the best athletes usually keep quiet. The loud people, the mediocre, are usually subpar compared to those at the top. Why? Because they are too busy talking to get any real work done. If you want to be respected, let your actions do the talking. Remember, words are the cheapest commodity in life, while actions are the toughest.

50. **Set the best damn example for your children. Have character, self-discipline and work hard** ~ This saying is meant for everyone, even those without children. Many of us have no motivation, or temporary motivation. Many of us just don't care how we act or what our character is like because we often have no one relying on us but ourselves. It's time to change that. Think of your children, or future children. Every day ask yourself, "Would I want my kid to look up to me?" and, if the answer is "No," change. It takes a lifetime to develop greatness in character and be virtuous, so start now! Be the role model for our younger generation and your offspring.

51. **The success of every man comes from the woman behind him** ~ It's no secret that behind every successful man is the woman who keeps him grounded. Often in life we need someone by our side who will be there for us in the dark and help us break down barriers. One of the greatest gifts of your life will be the person you marry. You shall use this power with great force, as it can either make you or break you. Don't accept just any partner; never stop searching until they meet your standards.

52. **The world and everything in it can be yours if you are willing to work hard as hell in your younger years** ~ It takes a lifetime to achieve greatness. But not just any lifetime—an average life will never result in greatness. You must live the life of a legend. Pick an industry and be relentless on your way to the top while sacrificing every other part of your life for a few years. This is how you dominate. Too many older people look back on their lives with regrets and realize they wasted a lot of time. Don't let this be you. The whole world can be yours if you put in the work now for the future. How do you start? Pick an industry, learn everything in it, meet everyone you can, and find the top person in that field. Study them and then outwork them.

53. **Every success story starts with someone who decided to take action** ~ Are you one of those people who love to talk about success? You have these wild imaginations for what you want, but they stay in your sleep. You can talk and dream about success all you want, but until you take action, nothing is going to get done. You can over-indulge yourself with other people's success stories, but when are you going to write your own? Do you believe that person would be where they are today if they only dreamed of success? They busted their ass each day to get to where they are.

54. **Success doesn't happen overnight, it's created through hard work every day** ~ Some people think that success happens overnight, but there's no such thing. Unless you win the lottery or inherit a fortune, overnight success doesn't happen. People don't want to go through the pain of discipline and sacrifice to become successful. They want success now. When starting a business, you need to think, "Is this sustainable for long-term success?" If you're caught up in the moment and not in the future, you're going to end up failing. Your actions compiled each day over ten years are going to determine if you're successful or not.

55. **Winners make a habit of doing things losers don't want to do** ~ Nothing separates a person more than the habits they possess. Habits are the foundation of who we are, what we do, and how we do it. Look at any loser or winner in life, then look deeper. What is each of them doing day to day? You will find that the winners of life have habits that make them winners. They wake up early, don't waste time and they make sure every hour of their day is put to good use. While life's losers do the opposite. They float through the day, and waste all their free time. Change your habits and it will change your life.

56. **They only talk about you because if they talked about themselves, nobody would listen** ~ When starting any endeavor for the betterment of yourself, people will laugh at you. Most of the time this will be behind your back. These are the same people who have never taken risks in life. They've decided they want to bring you down to their level, but don't fall for it. People get scared because you're doing better than them and that makes them feel weak. With every level you jump in life, the more people will talk about you. They're so busy focusing on you that they don't realize how average they live. It makes them feel good, but doesn't do any harm to a Lion. When you get wind of people talking about you, you know that you're doing something right. Continue to block out the noise of these people and focus on building your empire, leaving them behind.

57. **Surround yourself with people who are going to push you to greater heights** ~ Everyone has a choice of whom they surround themselves with. Most people still have the same friends from high school. This is a key indicator you aren't growing. If you hang around employees, you'll be there next. The same goes if you surround yourself with millionaires. Find people who are comfortable telling you how it is. Too many people are scared of telling the other person how they feel because it'll hurt their feelings. The world has amounted to giving first-place trophies to kids who come in last. You need to be wary of who you spend your time with. Do whatever it takes to surround yourself with those who are going to make you a better person and force you to become great.

58. **Only those who see the invisible can do the impossible** ~ Every invention you see in the world today started with an idea. Elon Musk saw a world full of cars running on electricity instead of oil. Do people call him crazy? They still do. He took the world he saw and made it a reality. If you want to achieve something extraordinary in your life, don't be afraid to do the impossible. You've had ideas for a business, but someone told you it wasn't going to work out. You let them get the better of you. Do you know where the wealthiest place in the world is? The graveyard. Is that where you want your idea to end up?

59. **It doesn't matter how slow you go, you're still beating everyone who's on the couch** ~ As long as you are moving and you are actually working on your goals, you are beating the losers who do nothing. Remember that. The journey of success is hard as hell; the journey to the top is ruthless. Every morning, when you awake just know that there are millions sleeping late and getting nothing done. Think of this whenever you feel down or you think you are continuously 'falling' or going 'too slow.' Of course, use this type of motivation on your off days. On your good days, focus on your competition, and I guarantee you they are not on the couch. You have to know their work schedule and then outwork them!

60. **All of our dreams can come true if we have the courage to pursue them** ~ Do you remember when you were a kid and everything was amazing? You had these dreams of becoming anything you wanted. Then one day, your parent, teacher, or friend told you that you couldn't achieve your dreams. They laughed at you and said "It's time to get back to reality." You believe them and for what? Don't let that one instance with that person deter you from chasing your dreams. As you go through life, there will be dream killers all around you. These are people who've already given up on their life. Understand that it is possible to achieve your dreams if you have the courage to start. You only have one life, what do you really have to lose?

61. **No masterpiece was ever created by a lazy artist** ~ Do you think we'd know Leonardo da Vinci if he was lazy? The concepts he taught and discovered by himself are still used today. You can be the greatest athlete in the world, but if you're lazy, there will come a day when you meet someone who has worked harder than you. They'll embarrass you and leave you wondering where it went wrong. If you want to be great at anything, it's a constant practice of repetition. Pablo Picasso worked on his craft every day. Bill Gates never took a day off in his 20s. If you want to leave your mark on the world, start by figuring out what you love to do and do it better than anyone else.

62. **Do what you can, where you are, with what you have** ~ You are where you are in life because of you. Sure, upbringing and circumstances may have shaped you, but ultimately your life is made by you. You can't change the past, but you have the ability to change everything else in your life. It doesn't matter if you are homeless, a millionaire, a cook, a maid—do what you can, with what you have, to get ahead now. Circumstances, excuses and your complaints mean nothing to anybody. People don't care and neither should you. Whatever your vision or goal is, work like hell towards it every day. If that means you need to sacrifice a lot, so be it. Don't live for temporary pleasure, live for eternal greatness.

63. **Your future is only uncertain when it's in someone else's hands. Make your own moves** ~ Whenever you believe that 'someone else will take care of me' or 'I'm safe in my job,' you are allowing people and things outside of your control to determine your future. It's time to take control of your life. If you work a day job, start earning a side income. If you are in school, read more books than required to get and stay ahead. Make it a priority to meet and network with successful people. It's your life and you need to make your own moves.

64. **I've always been one to invest in myself rather than going to the club** ~ Do you go out and party on the weekends, wasting three or four nights a week on short-term pleasure? Are trying to drown at the misery of your life? You don't have the confidence to ask a girl out when sober? These will never be the characteristics of a Lion. Have you ever stopped and thought why you're unhappy with your life? It's because deep down you know you deserve more than the life you're currently living. It starts with investing in yourself. Go to seminars, buy books, take courses, hire a coach, and surround yourself with like-minded people. If your friends go out and party, it's time you find new friends. Don't give in to the average lifestyle, you're destined for more.

65. **Do not be a slave to your emotions; have absolute control over them** ~ If you can master yourself, you can master and control others easily. The greatest battle of our life is within our own mind. If you want to reach the top and become legendary, you must be able to control your urges and temptations and do what you have to do regardless of what you feel like doing. You cannot let the cloud of anger or the feeling of being horny get in your way. You must stay objective and act with reason and logic. Then, and only then, can you master yourself and dominate your life and your competitors.

66. **Write your name and add 'The Great' to it. What would 'The Great' version of yourself be doing differently than you do now?** ~ Have you ever wondered what you would be like while living life to your fullest potential? Take an analysis of yourself right now: your habits, routines, schedule, and friends. Will they lead you to greatness or will they make you remain average? Now ask yourself, what would your habits, routines, and friends be like if you added 'The Great' after your name? One of the reasons super successful people become successful is because they think they are successful before they actually are. They study the habits of the Greats and implement them into their own life. Every day, think of yourself as Your Name + The Great and then do whatever it is that the legendary version of you would do and you will certainly become a legend yourself.

67. **If you want to achieve greatness, stop asking for permission** ~ Stop asking everyone else if you're going to be successful. You can read all the books, have the best coaches, attend every seminar, and still not become successful. You have to know within yourself that you're going to do whatever it takes. No one is going to hand you greatness and you certainly can't take a pill for it. Greatness is achieved over a lifetime. Julius Caesar didn't ask anyone if it was okay to start a civil war. He just went after Pompey because he knew it would give him ultimate power. Don't wait for your teachers or parents to tell you that you're special. You have to start on your own and start today!

68. **Believe so much in yourself that nothing is going to stop you** ~ Everyone who has ever become successful has been doubted in their life. The abilities they shared with the world were put to shame. Someone starts a business and fails. They let that one failure define their entire life. You have to brush the dirt off and get back up, because you have more battles to fight. Believe so strongly in what you're doing that there's no such thing as failure. You only fail when you quit. Some people may call you cocky, even arrogant; they're jealous of your self-confidence. Become massively successful in the face of those who said you couldn't do it. When obstacles come up, figure out a way to get through them.

69. **If you don't have the money or the connections, your only choice is to outwork everyone** ~ Control what you can control in your life. Some people may be born rich, have great genetics and a huge, well-connected family, while others have nothing. It's not your fault where you start but it's your fault where you end. While you are young, you should have the mindset that every day when you wake up, "No one is going to outwork me." Don't just talk about your grind, live by your grind. Put in the work now because every minute of the day is precious when you are starting at the bottom.

70. **Hang out with those people who will push you to be better** ~ The people you spend your time with have a huge impact on who you will become. When you hang out with people who have no work ethic, goals, or dreams you will not become the strongest version of yourself. Cut out the losers, people with bad habits, complainers and whiners. Find winners: People who are driven, have a vision for their life, accompanied by a work ethic to get them there. And if you can't find anyone, be by yourself and work by yourself until you do.

71. **Work hard in silence and let success be your noise** ~ There's going to come a time in your life when you don't need to share what you're doing. In the beginning, it can be invigorating. You wish to share your ideas with the world. Over the course of time, you'll learn that people question what you're trying to accomplish even if you've already been successful. If you want to share your accomplishments? Share them once they have been completed. This keeps people off balance and wondering what you're going to do next. Let your success speak for you. Until then, don't stop working.

72. **You did not wake up today to just be average** ~ Success isn't something that'll come to you overnight. It's a compilation of your day-to-day actions. You may think it's okay to take a day off to relax, to watch the football games. This is what the average person tells themselves, but you're better than them! You go golfing a few times per week, but don't understand why you aren't successful. These are luxuries that you can afford once you are successful. What is one action, one step you can take today that's going to get you a better tomorrow? Focus on creating content and providing as much value as you can day in and day out. Soon enough, success will come your way.

73. **True greatness can never be reached without obsession** ~ It's hard as hell to reach greatness. It's a category that is given only to the people at the top, the legends. So many of us want to become Great, yet very few are actually on their way. To become Great, you must understand and be willing to work multiple hours every day solely on your craft... and then some more. You can never let the thought of 'I'm tired' or 'I don't feel like it' stop you. Those are the excuses that the average person likes to use. The choice is yours, are you willing to obsess over your vision until it's a reality?

74. **Always stay hungry and never be satisfied with your current accomplishments** ~ On your journey, there will be times when you succeed. You should be celebrating these accomplishments, but only for a short amount of time. If you take too much time celebrating, you're going to lose your momentum. What you had just accomplished is excellent. However, it's going to seem small a year or two from now. If you are consistently growing and building your business to new heights, you can never be satisfied. This is an attitude you must take with you your entire life. There will always be someone behind you who has what you want; don't give them too much time to take it.

75. **Use your pain to push you to greatness** ~ We all have a chapter we don't read out loud. They were dark times in your life. You have two choices, to play victim or use it as motivation for a better life. If you use your dark time as fuel to get you to a better place, you become unstoppable. You get fired from your job, so it's the perfect time to start the new business you've been putting off. Create a new story for yourself, one that you can tell your children. Enduring tough times is common, playing victim is common. You wouldn't be common if you're reading this book. Take charge of your life, you're more powerful and resilient than you think.

76. **We all have the same 24 hours. Your success is dependent on how you use the 24** ~ It doesn't matter who you are, where you live or what your lifestyle is like, we all have the same 24 hours in a day. The people at the top plan out their days, weeks, months, and stay consistent in their routines. Are you broke and unmotivated and just want things to be handed to you? Then I guarantee you spend your day wrong. If you are not where you want to be, study successful people and change to their habits one by one. Don't pretend you don't have enough time if you are not successful. The people at the top work 24/7 and don't stop when it gets tough. Learn from them and one day you will become them.

77. **Let the fools scream and argue. A real man is in control of himself, always** ~ Yelling doesn't make you strong and anger doesn't make you tough. They only make you look like a fool, someone who can't handle themselves. Those who yell all the time are not respected. People just get used to it and then ultimately resent you for it. Instead, be cool, calm, and collected as the old saying goes. The person who can be cool under pressure while everyone else is choking is the leader. That person is the only one capable of getting sh*t done in a timely fashion. That's the person people look up to and respect. Don't be a loud mouth. Be the leader of your pack.

78. **Your greatest asset: Doing the things that others won't** ~ Everyone talks a good game. They'll have you believing they're changing. Yet, their actions don't coincide with their words. They're out partying. When you ask them about their business, they become irritated. If you wish to be successful, you must be willing to leave everyone. People are afraid of being alone, that's why they hate their life. If you follow what everyone else is doing, you'll live the life like everyone else. Be in love with the grind and the betterment of yourself. Get up early, earlier than everyone else. Be willing to work weekends. If you repeatedly do the things that other's won't do, you're already on the road to success.

79. **If you don't believe in yourself, why is anyone else going to believe in you?** ~ You have to be the biggest motivator of yourself. Especially when you're starting, people will tell you that you can't do it or laugh at you. Don't let their limiting beliefs hold you back. How are you supposed to sell others on your vision when you don't believe in yourself? You know what you're doing is good or bad. If you're just in it for the money, the people around you will be able to sense it. People don't have to believe in your dreams for you to accomplish them. But in the end, you must give them a reason to see why they shouldn't have underestimated you.

80. **Don't look down upon people. Treat the janitor with the same respect as the CEO** ~ One of the best qualities of a super successful person is their ability to get along with everyone. In business, you must be able to put your bigotry, biases, and opinions aside. Keep them to yourself. There is no room for them. Treat everyone with respect until they prove they don't deserve it. Never look down on someone, whatever their job is, because you don't know where they will be in a few years. Only idiots build barriers by making fun of others because they feel superior. Start showing others respect, and your opportunities will multiply.

81. **The harder the battle, the sweeter the victory** ~ There is nothing more satisfying in this world than achieving victory through hard work and dedication. You have a goal in your mind for months, then comes the moment when you hit a breakthrough and achieve it. To achieve the goal, you must put in the blood, sweat, and tears. The greatest battle will be fought between your two ears. You haven't accomplished this goal before, so therefore you think you can't do it. That's bullsh*t! If you work long, smart and hard enough, anything can be yours. This is not for the weak. There will be sleepless nights. Times where you desperately wish to give up. Despite it all, you were able to prevail to the sweet side of victory.

82. **Be all in or get all out when it comes to your goals. There is no halfway** ~ There are two segments of the population: Those that write goals and those that don't. By writing goals, you are already in the top 10%. But what separates the 1% from the 9% is that they go all out. They don't write a goal just to write one, they write that goal to absolutely destroy it. Get into the habit of writing goals that are within your grasp, and have your vision be the one that's hard to reach. If you plan your milestone goals out and always hit them, you will certainly reach your vision. No excuses, no 'not enough time'... it's all bullsh*t. You need to take control of your life and be willing to work like hell to make your vision a reality. Go all in with your goals.

83. **Learn to say "No" without explaining yourself** ~ "No" is one of the most powerful words invented, yet hardly anyone uses it. When you don't want to do something, or hang out with someone, a simple "no" is perfectly acceptable. It's also powerful. It shows that you do not need to explain yourself and you will not be persuaded to go against what you truly want to do. Whether people like that answer or not, they will respect it and respect you for being straightforward. Remember, this is your life. You call the shots and only you can decide if something has a place in your life.

84. **Be tougher than your life is and stronger than any situation** ~ The toughest people are made by the toughest situations. Tough people, people who can endure whatever life throws at them, are uncommon people. These uncommon people are those who can say no to temporary pleasure and fix the 'massive problems' that people face. Not because they are smarter, but because they don't back down. Control your life and do not let it control you. Always be above any situation and have the grit and perseverance to weather any problem, big or small. Any time you back down or say 'I can't do it' or 'I don't feel like it,' you trigger a bad mentality. You must be strong for yourself, for your family and for your future vision.

85. **If you don't take risks, you'll work for someone who does** ~ Taking risks is necessary if you wish to live a desirable life. When you think of the top companies in the world, Amazon, Apple, Walmart, Starbucks: Do you believe those companies were able to grow as large as they are today because they didn't take risks? You're never going to fail. You either learn for the next time or you succeed. Taking risks makes life more exciting. You need excitement in your life. Feel the rush of adrenaline going after something you love. If it doesn't work out, you'll be able to overcome it. You need to believe in yourself and your capabilities more.

86. **It isn't your age or gender that predicts success, it's your mindset** ~ Nothing matters more in terms of success than your mindset. Your mind is your most powerful weapon; it can allow you to turn your dreams into reality or it can destroy them. Too many of us do not realize the impact of our present mindset. If you think you can't do something, you can't. If you think you can't wake up early or can't run your business profitably, you can't. If you think you're ugly, others will think so, too. But if you have absolute confidence in yourself and your abilities, you can achieve success. Before working on anything else in life, work first on your mindset. It's your best ally. Never lie to yourself, do what you say you will do, and keep yourself accountable.

87. **You can have results or excuses, not both** ~ What's one thing in common that every successful person has? They don't make excuses. They take 100% responsibility for their life. The average person lets their excuses get in the way. Even in the most dire circumstances, those who are successful look for a silver lining. They never make excuses as to why they aren't where they want to be in life. If something didn't work out, they get back up and push themselves much harder the next time around. You don't get results with excuses. You can only pick one. Which will it be?

88. **Be the type of person you would want your kids to grow up to be** ~ There should be no greater motivation for yourself than to want to provide the best possible life for your future family. More than that, become the number one role model for your children. When they think of you, make sure they think of a man of grit and persistence, who is level-headed, has self-control, works hard and gets the job done no matter the obstacle. Completing goals for yourself is motivating, but try having your motivation be your family or future family; now, that is really motivating. Routinely ask yourself, would I want my kids to admire me? Would I want my kids to be like me? If not, change.

89. **Leave the world a better place because you were here** ~ What impact do you want to have on the world when you're gone? Some want to leave money, others leave nothing. To have a lasting legacy, you need to have an impact on people, to be able to move people. People forget what you say, but won't forget how you made them feel. Are you creating content? Videos, books, and speeches that can be taught for centuries after you're gone. Think Napoleon Hill. Will your name live on for generations or be forgotten? The choice is up to you. How you go about your day, every day, will determine whether or not you die with a legacy.

90. **Be who you are, not who the world wants you to be** ~ Who were you before the world told you who you are? You had these grand ambitions that got torn up and thrown away. The people and circumstances around you make you believe you're not worthy of success. If you try to please everybody, you'll live with toxic shame and not be able to get anywhere. You'll say 'yes' to everything that comes your way. Understand that, no matter what you do, people are always going to dislike you. If you're an artist, be an artist. If you're an entrepreneur, be an entrepreneur. If you desire to be a teacher and help others, become a teacher. Don't let others define the life you should live. Be who you were meant to be.

91. **How can you ensure that you will be remembered after death? By attaching your name to an idea. For ideas never perish, only people ~** There have been over ninety billion people who have lived before you. They thought their names would never be forgotten. However, most are forgotten, except for the very few legends that are now icons. So how can you ensure that your name will stand throughout the test of time? By starting a business or a movement that is connected and started by you. The movement or business will go on well after your death and people will be able to see who you were and what you did. You need to think bigger than you are now and know that people connect more with an idea than with a person.

92. **You weren't born to just pay bills and die** ~ Isn't that a sad statement? Yet, it's one nearly every person in the world lives by. Don't you think you were destined for more? You can't keep wishing or not taking action because you'll end up like that statement above. Life was meant for excitement, adventure, meeting new people, falling in love and becoming the best version of yourself. You have so much to offer to the world. If you hold it back, there will never be a greater tragedy.

93. **If you want something you never had, you have to do something you've never done** ~ Conformity kills. It's a slow and painful death. You look up and have been working the same dead-end job for the last twenty years. Your marriage doesn't have the spark it once had, but you won't file the divorce papers. You don't believe it can get any better than you already have. This is a great lie. How would a new romance change your life? One where you're passionate about each other? Try starting a new career or going off on your own. Keep yourself on the edge. If you're not happy with where you are right now, change. Do something drastic you won't be able to get back. Move, quit your job, breakup with your girlfriend or boyfriend, or start a new relationship. Start implementing events that'll get you to your ideal state. These have to be events you've never done before.

94. **Believe you are the best in your industry before you actually are** ~ The true Greats of any industry have all thought they were the best long before they reached that level. Without their initial self-confidence and belief, they never would have gotten past the thousands of obstacles along their way. The countless hours and setbacks cannot be overcome from a wimpy or an average mindset. You need to have absolute faith you belong with the big boys, and that you can actually win against them. I challenge you to believe you are the top and then act like it every waking hour of the day.

95. **No matter how busy you may think you are, you must find time for reading, or surrender yourself to self-chosen ignorance** ~ Reading is the ultimate power source; that is, if you know how to use it. So many people complain that they don't know how to become successful, where to start, or what's the best path to take. Well, the answer is simple: Read. Read biographies, success books, and books on various subjects. Reading gives you the power to learn from the most successful people in the world: their grind, rise, and ultimate rule. If you waste most of your time watching TV and partying, then stop! And pick up a damn book. When you find an industry you know you want to become the best in, read every book on the subject. This is the fast-track to success.

96. **A young Lion is still a Lion** ~ In the modern world, age is not a factor in success. There are millionaires and billionaires in their 20s. There are legendary athletes in their 20s. There are world-renowned creatives in their 20s. To use the excuse 'I'm too young' or 'I'm too inexperienced' stops us from going after massive success. The key to success is having an obsessive mindset. A mindset that is so strong that the distractions will not distract you in the least bit. A mindset that has a clear vision. As long as you have the right attitude, you will become the Lion you were always meant to be.

97. **All of your dreams await just on the other side of your fears** ~ If you could have everything you ever wanted in the world, but you had to get out of your comfort zone, would you? The comfort zone is a terrible place to stay. Boats stay in the harbor, but that's not what they're made for. I understand it's not easy getting out of your comfort zone, but it's something every successful individual has had to do. If you won't grow, you'll never live the life you want. By starting little by little, you can begin to conquer your fears, no matter what it is. If you quit making excuses and stand toe to toe with your fears, you'll knock them out. If you want an amazing life, get ready to be uncomfortable.

98. **One day at a time, but keep your attention on the future** ~ Rome wasn't built in one day and neither will your business be. If you think you'll get success within a few months of starting your business, that couldn't be further from the truth. If you try and do too much at once, you'll burn out, which is worse than failing. Stay grounded in the moment and where you want to go. Set daily, weekly, monthly, quarterly, semi-annual, and yearly goals. Every goal you accomplish is a stepping stone towards a greater life. Think about the person you'll become once your goals are realized.

99. **Losers quit when they fail. Winners fail until they succeed** ~ The only way you can fail in life is if you quit. If circumstances present themselves that will try to break you, become resilient. Are you ready to take yourself more seriously? To understand you are a winner, no matter what society or the school system says? The people you look up to in the world kept trying over and over again until they succeeded. They didn't let anyone or anything deter them. You need to do the same.

100. **Ancient empires were grown by wars, battles and violence. Modern empires are grown by businesses, acquisitions and deals** ~ It's a new world filled with much better opportunities than our forefathers ever dreamed of. There is no more 'birthright' to wealth, fame, and power as there was in ancient times. And if there is, it is far less than it once was. We are living in a golden age for those who know how to use it. The world we are a part of has millions of opportunities. Most of those opportunities are found in business. To build a modern-day empire, you must learn modern-day empire-building skills: negotiating, strategic thinking, timeless laws of success, accompanied by absolute knowledge of your industry. The other part of the equation? You must have a massive vision, killer work ethic and an insatiable desire for greatness.

101. **The bad news: Time flies. The good news: You're the pilot** ~ Time is the only commodity you can't get back. Once it's wasted, it's gone forever. Think about how many more hours you'd be able to spend on your business if you didn't go out partying every weekend. Instead of watching TV, you read a book. You're in control of your time, protect it wisely. People will constantly be trying to take it from you. They'll want to delegate tasks to you that take away from the big picture. We all have the same amount of time to work each day, how come some people are more successful than others? Because they know what and how to spend their time on tasks that matter to their success.

102. **Dress like you own the bank, not like you need a loan from one** ~ You can't change the looks you were born with, but you can enhance your clothes, style, and attractiveness. What you look like is the first thing people notice and judge you on. Other people don't matter as much as you do. You should dress well because you have self-respect. Every day you get out of the house: comb your hair, take a shower, and dress smart. A suit or dress is not necessary, but dress for the occasion, and then a little more. When you wear nicer things, you feel better about yourself and your productivity level increases. Dress smart. It's how people judge you and it tells others how you feel about yourself without saying a word.

103. **When I wake up in the morning I have two goals: Change the world and have one hell of a good time** ~ When you wake up in the morning, what do you think of? Are you thinking about how much you hate your job? Or are you thinking how you can break free from that job? The first few hours will determine how the rest of your day goes. Do you have a reason for getting up? What are your objectives? The Lions of the world know what they are going to accomplish each day. If you let others take control, you're not going to live your ideal life. What do you want to do? That shouldn't consist of answering emails; it should consist of providing values to others. Make sure you're having fun with it. It's not going to be all glorious, but they'll be silver linings. It's time you live life on your terms.

104. **Inside every self-made man is a poor kid who followed his dreams** ~ 88% of the top 1% weren't born there. They saw their life's situation and didn't want to put their kids and wife through it as well. Enough was enough. They ground and sacrificed. Others called them crazy, but they kept pushing through. Find out how they turned their lives around. Reach out to them for advice. Pay them if you have to. The self-made man wanted a life of his own, not a life others dictated for him. When life got tough, he didn't give up. He'd already hit rock bottom and used that motivation to reach the top. You don't have to let your current situation define how your future is going to be. You have the option each day to start the change of a better life.

105. **True freedom is to do what you want in life without the worry** ~ At the end of the day, everyone is chasing freedom. There are different types of freedom, however. Freedom from your job, freedom from your bills, freedom from your bad habits. Freedom isn't being able to quit your job and play golf every day. Over time, your life will become complacent and you'll become unhappy. As a Lion, freedom means to live a life on your terms. You work the hours you wish. No one tells you when to come in or when to leave, you do as you please. You're able to travel or spend more time with your family. This also includes financial freedom so you no longer worry about not having enough. That is what true freedom means.

106. **It's bullsh*t when you say you 'don't have time.' If you really want something in this life, you'll make the time** ~ Too many people cannot 'find the time' to work on their dreams. But they 'find the time' for TV, social media, and staying up late. It's time to get serious about your life. Spend all your free time working on your vision. Cut out all the crap in your life. It's neither necessary nor helpful. It's a waste. Take yourself seriously and use your time to build your empire.

107. **My mom worked too hard for me to not be great** ~ If you've ever had a parent that was 100% for you, believed in you and in your dreams, you damn well owe it to them to make your dreams your reality. Success is your duty and you will make it happen no matter the circumstance you find yourself in. Parents who sacrifice so that their children can have a better life than they had are keepers and rare. Always remember that. You were born for greatness. And you are the only one who can make it your reality.

108. **If you want to be rich, learn how to build, buy or create assets** ~ The number one reason that people do not become rich is that they work for a paycheck. If you want to be rich, you need to use that money you make from your paycheck to invest in assets. An asset is something that puts money in your pocket without you directly working for it; for example, royalties from books or music, real estate holdings, businesses, etc. This is a foreign concept to most people, who just want a higher paying job or a job raise, but that just puts you in a higher tax bracket. Did you know assets are taxed at 0 to 20%, while a normal paying job is 40% and higher? But not many people know this. This is why the rich pay less in taxes than the poor and middle class. The school system purposely doesn't teach this type of financial education because they want robots who will do their job and that's it. Change your life and start making passive income.

109. **When I look back, I only have one regret: Not chasing my dreams sooner** ~ You're always going to be too old or too young to chase your dreams. You're never going to have the right financial standing or connections. These are self-made excuses that are holding you back from achieving your dreams. Age has no correlation to your success. There are teenagers who are making a full-time living. Then there's Colonel Sanders who founded KFC when he was in his 60s. There will come a moment when you run out of time. You could get in an accident today or an illness tomorrow. You can't expect you're going to live your entire life expectancy. The sooner you start, the earlier you'll achieve your desired success.

110. **Do not judge my story based on the chapter you walked in** ~ Every single person you meet has a story. They all have family, friends, problems and achievements. You should never judge a person based on who they are or what they are doing at the present moment until you get to know them. Many of us are in the 'lost identity' phase, not knowing what to do or who we are as a person. Some of us are in the grind stage, and just a few are at the level that everyone wants to be: massive success. The moral is: Don't judge people, for in a few years they could be completely different persons. A loser could become powerful and a powerful person could become a loser. Respect everyone while focusing on yourself and on your priorities.

111. **Lower your standards for no one. Keep to your habits and live by your own life's philosophy** ~ Lions do not follow the crowd. They are true to themselves and live by their own life's philosophy. They embrace their individuality and do not need a crowd to boost their ego. They are not sheep that need to be a part of a herd to feel safe. Lions are mavericks. If you love waking up early, but you have a partner or friends who like to stay up late and wake up late, f*ck them. It is that simple. You are doing what is best for you. You do not change your habits for anyone and everyone just to make them feel comfortable. You are in a game of success that requires focus on you and your journey. Be true to yourself.

112. **Never be ashamed of your insecurities. Wear them like armor and they can never be used against you** ~ You cannot change the way you look, where you came from or the genes you were given from birth... But you can change everything else. People become very insecure and uncomfortable when their flaws are highlighted. You truly cannot do anything about the looks you were given. Just stay fit and clean. Besides that, know that you are you. We are not soft, and it needs to be said. Any flaw or insecurity you have, own it, it's yours for life. It's you and it's always going to be you. When people talk about it, don't shy away and feel belittled, speak and say 'Yeah, I do, it's who I am.' You need to be comfortable in your own skin. Control what you can control in life, such as: mindset, strength, discipline, vision, and work ethic, just to name a few. Don't waste time on trying to fix your born 'flaws' with superficial fixes. The cure is to openly accept your flaws and move on.

113. **You're rewarded in public for what you do in private** ~ Have you ever found yourself saying, "Look at how successful that person is. I wish I could be like them." What you might not understand is what that person went through. The early mornings and late nights. Their friends and family telling them that they can't do it. The years of grinding while everyone else is having a good time or partying. Giving up their weekends. You're signing a contract if you want to be successful. If you're starting a business to have more freedom, be careful. The first few years or decades, you can't stop trying to master the art of your craft. There's no difference between you and me. The hard work that you put in today will be glorified in the future.

114. **What's better than being in love? Being in love with someone you can build an empire with** ~ Find someone who will motivate you and make you better, someone who wants to build something with you. They do not have to have the same skill set, personality, or position in life. They just need to have the ability to understand you, share the same mindset and vision for the future. This kind of 'power couple' is rare, so if you ever find it, think twice before letting it go. What holds these two together, more than anything, is their long-term plan and vision. Something that they envisioned together and will make a reality by a team-effort. And to build a true empire will take a lifetime, which is how long a true relationship should last. Nothing is more powerful than your spouse, so choose your relationships carefully and stay loyal.

115. **The days you don't want to are the days you have to** ~ Just f*cking do it. Legends have never been made by setting goals and then making excuses for why they aren't accomplished. That's a loser's habit and one most people share. Legends write audacious goals and then they get them done. There is no 'maybe' in their heads. If they write it down, they will make sure it's done, even if that means sacrificing everything else in their life. You must be relentless with your goals. The world needs more legends and there is a legend inside of you waiting to come out. But you must act and finish what you start... No matter how you feel.

116. **Be careful who you trust, the devil was an angel** ~ Watch what you say and who you say it to. There are people who want to take advantage of your success. These are people who tell you about a 'great' business idea that only suits them. If you say too much to your competitors, they can copy what you're doing and make it even better. Everyone doesn't need to know everything about you. Most of the time it's better to keep your mouth shut. If someone asks you a question that you don't feel comfortable about answering, say, 'Maybe another time.' You're going to lose friends and you will make enemies. Success does strange things to people, be wary.

117. **Never confuse friendship with business. Business is all about the money and power** ~ Too many friendships are lost because of business. So many people go into business with their friends and end up regretting it. Why? Because business is not a joke, it's not a fun night out with the guys. It's about money, it's about profit, and it's about power. You need to understand that and, if you choose a partner, they need to understand that as well. You need to know your responsibilities and you both need to be committed. Most of your friends will not make the cut. They will be screw-ups. They will be liabilities. Leave your friends for when you want to have fun, and leave business to those who understand the game and all that it entails.

118. **If the Egyptians built pyramids without machines, you can build a business without excuses** ~ People who make excuses and complain about their situation will never be winners. Excuses mean nothing. We hear them, pretend to sympathize with the person, and then move on while thinking the other person can't bring to the table what they said they would. Never make another excuse again. The fact is that people are doing what you do today better than you are. And if that is true, which it is, then there is room for improvement and learning. Whatever your craft, business, or occupation is, be the best at it. Do whatever you have to do and more to get the job done and done right. In the game of success, the only people who make it are the people who feel their failures and successes in life are their responsibility. Not their team's, but theirs. Have that sort of mindset and watch your future grow.

119. **If you can't stop thinking about it, don't stop working for it** ~ Why would you even think about giving up on your dreams? If you don't give up, you can never fail. If you give up now, you'll spend an entire lifetime in regret. When walking down the street, most people look hollow. No one is smiling or enjoying life. They're thinking about their past failures or what they don't look forward to in the future. Keep pushing forward each day. Take time to appreciate all that you have done, but never be satisfied. There will come a day when everything you worked towards will come to fruition.

120. **Sometimes you have to risk it all for a dream only you can see** ~ As long as you have a clear vision for yourself and your future, no one else's opinion matters. Who cares what the sheep think? It's your damn vision. A vision is something each of us has at some point in our lives, a dream of something better than what we have now. The difference between that vision becoming your reality and its staying in your mind is action. Every day you must be putting in the necessary work, and then some more. Break down your vision into yearly, monthly, and weekly goals. As long as you're hitting your milestones, you will live your dream, and the whole world will see your vision.

121. **Do what you have to do until you can do what you want to do** ~ Are you ready to do whatever it takes to become successful? You can't spend lavishly or waste time on the weekends. You're going to have to keep your expenses low. There's no need for the luxurious cars or extravagant houses. You can acquire these possessions after years of hard work, if you're able to pay for them with your assets. People will question you; are you ready to answer their questions? You're going to have to make sacrifices. The sacrifices you make today are going to pay dividends in the future. Put your head down and continue working.

122. **A mentor is the shortcut to success** ~ Get a mentor. There is no 'maybe'... a mentor will jumpstart your success. But not just any mentor, find someone who is massively successful in what you want to do in life. Then, learn everything you possibly can from them. Work for free, try to go to all their meetings, and always ask questions. Successful people love ambitious young men and women. But you must step up and show them that you are ambitious. I started my first business at 19, failed at it for 4 months, found a mentor in that industry (the top person) and then made 6 figures by the end of the year. This is the power of finding a mentor. Don't try to do it all yourself. You are not the expert... yet.

123. **Some prefer to trade hours for dollars. I prefer to trade ideas for millions** ~ Why work for money when you can have money work for you? This is the way passive income works. Working a salary or hourly job can only get you so far. A job on commission is limitless, as is passive income. The common mindset today is that you have to work for your money. It's entirely possible to make money while you sleep. You can create a blog, drop-ship products, sell a product; the ideas are plentiful. This is 2017. The Internet is only going to get better, there's no reason why you can't be making money online right now. Once your side income grows bigger than your normal income, you can finally escape the rat race.

124. This may piss you off: You are where you deserve to be in life ~ Some of you are not going to like this, some will hate it but, it is the truth. We are all born in different situations, with different upbringings, experiences, and privileges. Some people are born with great genetics, rich families and have everything in the world, while some have nothing. We cannot choose where we come from. The only choice we have is how we are going to live our life. The fat person can easily become ripped. The poor man can easily become wealthy. When I say easily, I mean it is very possible with the right mindset. Stop feeling sorry for yourself. Self-pity is for losers and no one truly cares what you are feeling, especially if you are not successful. Take control of your life and realize you are where you are because of you. You have the power to change your life story right now...Become the legend you were supposed to be.

125. They may hate us together, but they can't stop us ~ As a power couple, you'll be hated in every way possible. Take Sarah Blakely and Jesse Itzler: People are going to be envious of them. It's not so much that people hate you; rather they wish they could have what you have. They're in a relationship with a partner that isn't feasible for their success. You come along and they become jealous. Your partner is going to determine whether you're successful or not. When you find the one, you can't be stopped.

126. They call us dreamers, but we're the ones who don't sleep ~ At night, I can't sleep. I sit there lying awake. This isn't from insomnia; it's from the idea of how I can make an impact on the world. There will come a time in your life where you don't wish to sleep because it's going to take you away from what you love to do. When this happens to you, understand that you're on the right track. The time for doing something that you hate is over. This is your life, not someone else's. What have you always dreamed of doing, but have held back? This is speaking in realistic terms. What's your ideal occupation? What would you do every day if money didn't matter? These are good starting points on your journey towards success.

127. **When you start winning, they start wanting** ~ We live in a socialistic world. With social media, people can contact you from all different avenues. As you acquire success, people are going to ask you how you made it. If you must, go in-depth with this person. People generally want the easy road to success; they don't want to see what you really have to go through. Be careful who you give your advice to. Your time is your most valuable asset. Is that person going to take what you said and implement it in their life? Those are the people you want to help, not the people who keep consuming and don't care to produce.

128. **Never let anyone get comfortable disrespecting you** ~ How people treat you in private, but especially how people treat you in public is important. Never allow someone to make a habit of disrespecting you in public, among your peers and or elders. If they do, other people will automatically think it's okay to disrespect you as well. They will think less of you. The solution? Break their knees. What I mean by that is tell them strongly and quietly to their face one on one that you will not tolerate disrespect. And, if they continue, know their weaknesses and exploit them.

129. **Be the somebody nobody thought you could be** ~ People are going to doubt you time and time again. I remember giving my first speech and having the people laugh at me when I told them my goals and dreams. This was in March 2016, when Become The Lion was just beginning. I've used that fuel to push me ever since. You have to show everyone how resilient you are. Just because they don't believe in you doesn't mean that you can't accomplish it. Enough of this bullsh*t—be who you were meant to be. Show up every day to go to war against yourself and the people around you. If you continue to take consistent action each day, compounded over time, the odds of becoming successful are heavily favored towards you.

130. **It's not Mondays that suck, it's your job** ~ Monday should be your favorite day of the week. It's the start of the week, the time to make weekly goals, and the time to build your empire stronger and more profitable than the week before. Now, if you hate Monday's, it's not the day that is bad, it's your lifestyle. And if you need to work at a job you hate, make sure when you get home or before you go to work you are grinding on your side hustle until you can make it your main hustle.

131. **Work until you no longer have to introduce yourself** ~ When you walk into a room, do you want to be another person or someone that everyone knows? The only way you're never going to have to introduce yourself is to become an expert in your industry. In the beginning and most of your time, you're not going to be known. But, over time, you become an authority figure, one people can look up to for advice. You can't expect to only put in a few hours each week and have everyone know your name. When you consistently put content out in the world that provides value each year, your name will be known.

132. **A woman's loyalty is tested when her man has nothing, a man's loyalty is tested when he has everything** ~ There is no better feeling than having found love before you are both successful. Why? Because you both have a vision for the future and you both support each other through the massive grind that is necessary for success. A woman will be tested when her man is poor and struggling, for she could be with many other men of wealth and power. And many women will leave. But the ones who stay and cheer you on and pick you up when you are down are keepers. And men, after that massive success, you will be tested by the many gold diggers. But always remember who was there during your grind. That woman is irreplaceable.

133. **People always make a list of what they want, yet they never make a list of what they're willing to give up** ~ To get what you want in life, you must be willing to give up temporary pleasure and commit to grinding. I don't know any person that has never wanted to be successful, yet so few actually achieve and live their ultimate vision... Why? Because they are not able to see that their present lifestyle will never allow them to become a massive success. Right now, make a list of things and habits that you need to get rid of in order to become a legend, a massive success. Then commit to getting rid of them. It will be hard, but necessary.

134. **I'd rather be a CEO at a small company than work for someone at a big company** ~ You have one life and in this life you need to be making your own moves. Making your own moves requires that you are working for yourself or for a company that you truly believe in. So many people want to be their own boss but don't know how to do it. The answer is out there: Take online courses, take classes at colleges, learn from mentors and read books while applying that knowledge. There is a multi-million dollar company inside each and every one of us. You just need to be willing to grind like hell for it.

135. **I've been one to forgive, but never to forget** ~ I will never forget what they said about me. They laughed at my goals and aspirations. The system said I'd never amount to much. But now, they all want to know how I did it, friendly than ever. I don't hold any grudges against them; rather, I feel satisfaction. Have a long memory and remember everyone who was and wasn't there for you. Michael Jordan forgave the critics, but he never forgot them. He used them as his motivation in the off season. There was never a dull moment in his life. Use those who doubt you as motivation to push yourself.

136. **I'd rather grind for five years than be a slave for 60** ~ Would you rather spend the next five years of your life grinding, or would you rather spend 60 years working for someone else? If you're willing to put in the time now, you're going to be able to live the life you wish. You're going to have to give up partying and sleeping in. Get rid of the negative people in your life. It's you against yourself. Are you trying to become a better person than you were yesterday? If you stay complacent, you're not going to live the life you want. You have to be in it for the long haul. You don't want to just become successful, you want to maintain that success throughout your life.

137. **Maturity doesn't come from age, it comes from experience** ~ Throughout history we can learn some eternal truths. Many of the richest and most powerful men and women started young. Alexander the Great conquered the known world by 32. Mark Zuckerberg was a billionaire by 23. The fact is that age has nothing to do with success and worldly wisdom. It is about the amount of time you spend on your craft, learning, experiencing, and evolving. Make sure you always spend your time wisely and look at every minute of the day as an opportunity to become wise and more experienced.

138. **The earlier you start, the earlier you succeed** ~ Wealth knows no age or sex, and it doesn't care about your story — it shows no sympathy and has no feelings. Know this, and whatever your age is right now, just start. As you get older, you will wish you had started younger. Put in the work now; promise yourself for one full year you will put in a crazy amount of hours every day on your craft or business. It's the choice of a Lion. You will never regret this choice. This decision will change you entirely and absolutely while taking you to places people only dream of. The time is now.

139. **The key to living like a King is to work like a slave** ~ Don't fool yourself. To live like a King or a Queen, you must first possess the work ethic of a slave. And when I say slave, I mean that you personally make the decision to work like hell for your dreams for about 10 years...10 years, it may seem like a huge time period, but in reality, it's short and absolutely worth it. During those years have three jobs, a side hustle, read books, have mentors and live the 'unbalanced life.' It's bullsh*t when people say you need balance. Balance is beautiful, but not until you get into a position in life where you want to be. It's stupid advice. It will only slow you down. Get serious. Right now.

140. **When people ask, "What do you do?", answer, "Whatever it takes."** ~ How badly do you want it? People are always talking about what they're going to do without taking action. 92% of New Year's resolutions fail because people talk about what they're going to do without having a plan. Develop the mindset that, no matter what happens to you, you're going to make it. There isn't any room for a backup plan. You have to be going at this 100%. There is no such thing as failure: You work until you succeed. Long nights and early mornings is what it's going to take. Sacrifice today for a better tomorrow. However long it takes, it's going to be well worth it.

141. **If you believed in Santa Claus for eight years, you can believe in yourself for five minutes** ~ How is someone supposed to believe in your idea or concept if you can't even believe in yourself? You aren't going to be able to believe in yourself if you stay on the sidelines. You develop confidence by taking action every day, doing things that scare the sh*t out of you. Getting out of your comfort zone is a must. You'll go through a lot of stages as an entrepreneur, but you're growing at each one. You're not going to be able to grow if you don't put in the work. Free time is the enemy. The more free time you have, the more you're going to doubt yourself. Plan your days, develop confidence, and anything can be yours.

142. **Make money. Use that money to make more money. Repeat** ~ If you want to make it big in this life, you need to fully understand this concept. When you make money from your job, do not go out and buy liabilities or things that don't put money in your pocket. Use your job's income to buy assets. Assets will make you more money than just keeping that money in the bank or wasting it on liabilities. The key: Use your income to invest in assets and over time your assets will pay for your lifestyle.

143. **Give me internet, a coffee, and a laptop, and watch me build an empire** ~ You don't need much to start an online business. Even if you only make a few thousand per month your first year, that's a comfortable living in a country such as Thailand. You're never going to truly be free until you create a business that makes you money while you're not working. You set up the systems that allow the money to come in whether you're working or not. Wouldn't it be nice to have a direct deposit coming in every day instead of every two weeks? This can be your life if you study the art of online marketing. You no longer need a brick-and-mortar business to make a living.

144. **We need more Lions and fewer sheep** ~ There are too many sheep running among us in society. Those are the people who want to stay average and don't want a comfortable life. When you wake up in the morning, you can decide to be a Lion or a sheep. Lions don't care for other people's opinions about themselves. Lions are in it to win it. They do whatever is necessary to become successful. Lions are at the top for a reason. Lions understand what it takes to be successful. Do you?

145. **My inspiration is who I will be 10 years from now** ~ Everyone should go watch Matthew McConaughey's Oscar speech. He said that his inspiration in life is not some other person, as it is with most of us. His inspiration is his future self. At 15, his inspiration was himself at 25. At 25, it was himself at 35, and so on. We are capable of so many great things in this life that we often get sidetracked by researching the greatest people of all time and feeling depressed because our life cannot compare. But instead of feeling lethargic, focus on who you will be in 10 years and always be progressing. You can be any person you want to be if you take consistent action.

146. **Don't rush into sh*t. Take your time and be massively strategic** ~ There are so many entrepreneurs who could become one of the Greats, if only they stayed consistent with their one business. As entrepreneurs, we get sidetracked by the next idea or venture and before we know it, we are a part of 3 to 5 businesses. This type of behavior is common and it can get you rich, but not very often ultra-rich. If you want to be one of the Greats, start planning out your every move. No more making decisions on the whim, such as: starting another business, partying that night, or getting in a relationship. Never get emotional. You need to weigh the pros and the cons in your head and see if that one decision is going to help or hurt your success... And that is how you get ahead, by making strategic moves in the right direction.

147. **There are plenty of obstacles in your path, don't allow yourself to become one of them** ~ Sometimes you need to take a step back on your journey and look around. Look at what you've accomplished and what you need to work on. Is there any area in which you know you're hurting yourself? This could be thinking that you can do design work when you're really a marketer. It could be super-hero syndrome and trying to do everything on your own. Don't blame others for why it's not working out and look at yourself. Are your actions, routines, and habits going to lead you to success? This isn't anyone's life, only yours. Take 100% responsibility for where you are in life and what you can do to change your current situation.

148. **What separates the good from the great is consistency** ~ How do you think someone becomes a huge success in anything that they do? The truth is, it doesn't matter what you think. What matters are the facts. And to be great in anything, you need to take consistent action dedicated to your craft every day. Anyone can do something every now and then or even a few times a week and become good. But good should never be your ideal. It should never be your aim. Being massively successful in one thing. You should be dedicating time every day towards it. Do not let emotions or the loser reason, 'I don't feel like it,' stop you. And if it does, you will never be great. In recap, pick that one thing. Do it every day and track your progress.

149. **You are what you do, not what you say you'll do. Remember that next time you speak** ~ Words are the cheapest commodity when it comes to success. Anyone can say or write whatever they want. Who they are going to be, what they are going to do, what they will be worth. But how many of us actually parlay our words into actions that produce real results? Few. It is a great idea to have an ideal version of yourself and to remember your dreams. But don't talk about them all the time to others without action. That is weakness that will make you look like a fool. I am sure you know someone who just talks, and nothing ever comes of it; don't be that person. Work in silence. Keep your mouth quiet and let your actions speak for your success. And as you are climbing the ladder of massive success, then, and only then, should you become a self-promoter.

150. **Motivation alone is bullsh*t; you need to be hungry and motivated** ~ **Motivation** is only temporary. Motivation will last you for hours or days but the true ingredient to everlasting success is hunger... A deep internal desire for more. You want more out of your life and you will not settle for half of your dreams and you will not live someone else's version of a 'good life.' That's why you need to be hungry every single day. You need to wake up every morning and say I am not going to bed until my goals for the day are f*cking done! No crybabies. No losers. Enough with the temporary ups and downs in your motivation and energy levels. Because being at the top of your industry requires that you are always on your game. Make a vision and work towards it, now!

151. **Live the life that people write novels about** ~ The bestselling books and movies are always about the greatness of the main character: Jay Gatsby, Gordon Gekko, Thomas Crowne, Scarface, The Godfather, etc. Be the main character in your own life's movie. Envision what you want and then go for it: Travel the world, become a professional athlete, become ultra-rich, do something profound for the global economy. Just be extraordinary. Chances are your favorite movies and books are your favorites because of the main character. You admire, are attracted by, and are allured by that person. You want to live his or her life, thinking you could never do that on your own. You are wrong. You are the sole creator of your own life's story. You can be whoever you want to be: watch all your favorite characters and then assimilate their best traits into your own. Be willing to change everything if that is what needs to happen. I did this a while back when I started in business, assimilating the traits from histories 'Super Greats.' Start now and live life on your own terms.

152. **Never make a decision when you're horny or angry** ~ If you want to be powerful, you must control your emotions. Powerful people are, in most cases, not born into power, but they discovered how to wield and grow their power by having complete control over their emotions. They do not make decisions when they are upset or in the presence of a person of the opposite sex. They make decisions based on facts, self-interest, and precision. They realize most people are trapped by their present 'feelings' or 'circumstances' and they use that to their advantage. Many powerful people exploit others by arousing their anger or manipulating them with sex, a con developed to get things out of the weak. Do yourself a huge favor and practice delayed gratification. Practice walking away in tense moments filled with different energies and emotions. Do not fall victim to what many people do every day. Play life on your own terms and manipulate the weak for your own benefit because, if you don't, the powerful will play you.

153. **The master has failed more than the beginner has tried** ~ Throughout history and now, there are people who are masters in their field. Many of us are quick to name those individuals as an 'overnight success' or 'born with that incredible ability, I wish I had that.' All of that is garbage and the talk of losers. What most people are blind to is that those now-masters put in a crazy number of hours, adding years of practice while overcoming many failures. And they pushed through their failures and made consistent progress. People do not like adversity, doing new things or adapting to change, which is why many stay beginners their whole life. You need to break this loser mindset in your own life. Start today—pick up something and stick with it. Mastery is not something you are born with, it is learned. Stop messing around. Start working on your craft and develop an iron will.

154. **Make your parents proud, your enemies jealous and yourself happy** ~ If you can live a life intertwined with all three of those concepts, it's going to be a life well-lived. Making my parents proud has always been a goal of mine. We take our parents for granted and don't realize how much they can help us. They have wisdom beyond our years. They might not believe what you believe in, but eventually they'll come around. You must never focus on your enemies, haters, or naysayers, but it does feel good when you prove them wrong. At the end of the day, it's about living a life that makes you happy.

155. **The most difficult roads often lead to beautiful destinations** ~ You may look at someone who's successful and wonder how they got there. They probably went through the University of Hard Knocks. If you read about successful people, almost every one of them failed in the beginning. Steve Jobs was fired from Apple. Henry Ford failed trying to create a racing car company. Both Jobs and Ford had an unrelenting drive to make the world a better place. There is light at the end of the tunnel. It may take a few years to see it, but eventually it'll happen. If you look at the NFL, it takes a few years before the rookies become experts. Take your time and be patient.

156. **If you're going through hell, keep going** ~ Even in your darkest hour, the sun will still shine. The sacrifices that you make today are going to lead to a better tomorrow. The sun is stuck behind the dampened clouds. You look and see a gray stillness in your future. One day, the sunshine breaks through. Everything you went through will all be worth it. See both sides of the coin. What you are going through to become successful is going to help you. You'll become more resilient and patient.

157. **It costs $0.00 to think like a millionaire** ~ The first step toward being a millionaire or billionaire is to start thinking like one. People flock around, spending money wherever and hoping their debit card accepts their purchases. We, as a society, do not keep track of our spending and we are in debt to the credit card companies. You need to realize that there is good debt and expenses, while there is also bad debt and expenses. We need to focus on building assets and limiting the buying of liabilities. Start investing in your financial intelligence today and read books about personal finance and economic history. Start dressing and acting better, act like the man or woman you ultimately want to become. Question yourself and ask if the strongest version of yourself would do this. Develop a ritual of tracking your spending and start a habit of reading 1 book per week about personal finance. This is a marathon, not a sprint. Stop acting poor and middle class, or you will forever be part of that socio-economic class.

158. **Never judge a book by its cover. An innocent beauty could also be the queen of an empire** ~ With wisdom comes the understanding that powerful people come in all shapes and sizes. Never underestimate someone based on their looks, style, or the way they act. Of course you can judge them, but never feel elitist towards them. They will only blind your judgment. Stay neutral. In the game of power; people may put on an appearance of innocence to get information out of you. You never know who you are talking to. Always be on guard when speaking to people and watch what you say. Respect others that you do not know, and never give them a reason to go to war with you over ignorant comments you might have said thinking you are above them. Powerful people can be 4 feet or 6 feet tall, woman or man, or even a child. With wisdom comes clarity.

159. **Being a true gentleman never goes out of fashion** ~ There's only one way to treat your lady and that's with the utmost respect. You may not agree on everything, but there will never be a need to raise your voice. If you are ever that mad, go for a walk and blow off the steam. The one thing money can't buy is how you treat others and how you treat others says a lot about yourself. Whether in public or private, you treat your girl as if she's your Queen and she'll treat you like a King.

160. **Push yourself because no one is going to do it for you** ~ In life, we rely on others. We believe others will make our dreams come true. What you might not understand is that people are going to let you down in your life. This is why you must rely on yourself. If you bet on yourself, you're never going to lose. No one is going to make you eat healthy; you have to take it upon yourself. No one will tell you to get up early or stop watching that show. 99% of the population won't try to understand what you're going after. They're not bashing your dreams, they just don't understand the concept. Remember, at the end of the day, all you have is yourself.

161. **The fact that you aren't where you want to be should be enough motivation** ~ People are always talking about motivation. There comes a point in everyone's life where motivational videos aren't enough. The motivation needs to come from within. If you don't like your f*cking job, do something about it! Quit being a little b*tch like the rest of the society. Get off your hands and knees and change. People get their feelings hurt too easily. We've become a much more sensitive world. What happened to the days of the past when 18-year-olds would be getting ready for war? Train yourself to be mentally tough!

162. **The goal isn't to live forever, it's to create something that will** ~ It's inevitable that you're not going to live forever. You can't take your money to the grave and a U-haul with your possessions won't show up to your funeral. You weren't put on this earth just to make money, you were put here to make an impact. So many people focus on the wrong things in life that lead them down a path to nowhere. Many wealthy people who only have money aren't satisfied with their life. Money will make you happy to a certain point. Make an impact that lasts forever and you'll become fully alive.

163. **Things that have been most valuable to me, I didn't learn in school** ~ I don't want to discourage you from getting an education. This isn't the question of whether or not to go to school. It's to have you understand that once you get out of school, whether high school or college, you must never stop learning. A formal education will only get you so far. Self-education is where your education can really take off. You can teach yourself the skills that it takes to be successful by reading and taking action. You can take courses on Udemy and acquire any skill you wish. YouTube is an excellent place to learn. There is tons of free content you can learn from. Just because you're out of school doesn't mean you should stop learning.

164. **My creed: Whenever I set a goal, I will get it done by the deadline or I will not sleep until it's completed. This formula is the key to success** ~ Enough with the bullsh*t goals, the goals that you write down but do not finish. There is no time for them when it comes to your personal success. Never set another goal until you promise yourself that you will follow through with it to its completion. It's life's losers who write their goals down every week and never accomplish them, not winners. The legends of business, sports, and other walks of life are those who can make audacious weekly goals, and finish them every week. They don't let people or 'circumstances' get in their way. They don't blame others, they blame themselves. They are the Lions. I write all of my goals down on Saturday morning and they are due Friday night; if I do not have them done, I stay up until they are. It's that simple.

165. **There is no shortcut; it takes time to build a better, stronger version of yourself** ~ If you want lasting success, it's not going to come to you overnight. Because once you learn the process, even if you fail, you'll still have that knowledge to start over. If you get off track, pull yourself back up. Success is something you want to maintain. Small changes in your day-to-day routine will give you a great ROI. Watch something that's going to stimulate your mind instead of pulling it down. It can be reading 10 pages of a book each day. It's creating these habits that are going to allow you to lead to the life you wish.

166. **If you want to be successful, you must learn to be comfortable being uncomfortable** ~ Make being uncomfortable a habit until you are comfortable doing anything. We only live once, and your time is limited, so don't be trapped by your fears. If you want to become the strongest version of yourself, you need to embrace your fears and things that put you on edge. The most successful people in the world became that way by putting themselves in situations where they were beginners... inexperienced, nervous, and anxious. They knew that by putting themselves out there, they would be massively uncomfortable, but the by-product of that would be tremendous confidence doing that same thing again. So, the next time you are fearful, act.

167. **Be strong, you never know who you're inspiring** ~ You may not think you're making progress, but even if you're inspiring just one person, that's all that matters. You don't know who's watching and that should give you more motivation to not give up. This could come from a friend or a family member. We all make mistakes; show the world how resilient you are. Be a role model to the entire world and share your story. There is someone who's going through the exact things you went through. They want to know how you did it—do you plan on letting them down?

168. **How many success stories do you need to hear before you make your own?** ~ The to-be successful read about successful people. They read and are inspired by their life stories. They sometimes find similarities and try to become that person in their entirety. But that type of motivation never lasts, and for a good reason. You are here to create your own life's story. Your own success story. One that people will look up to one day. And that happens not by pretending you are someone else, but by accepting your own individuality. The time is now for your light to shine, not tomorrow, not next year, NOW!

169. **Some say I'm showing off, other's say I'm inspiring. I guess it depends on what you're looking for** ~ You can take a wealthy person and become jealous of them, or you can applaud them because you know how hard they worked. How you feel about successful people is a direct reflection on yourself. You might've grown up believing the world is scarce. The truth is, there's an abundance, enough to go around and then some. Don't ever stop improving yourself because you're scared others will think of you differently. People questioned Elon Musk and Thomas Edison. Continue to be you while you go after your dreams.

170. **I'm not living the dream, I'm busting my ass to make freedom a possibility** ~ Getting to the top is the easy part. Staying there—well, that's the hard part. You should never speak the word retirement, because there will never will be a day when you quit. Maybe you slow down, but if you can't imagine doing what you're doing for the rest of your life, you need to find a different business to be in. Could you do what you're doing right now for another 50 years? When you grind day in and day out, even when you don't feel like it, that's what makes freedom a possibility.

171. **Study while others are sleeping. Work while others are lounging. Take action while others are wishing** ~ It's not too hard to become successful, at least compounded over time. Sleep is an essential part to your success, but it's liberating to start work when most people are waking up. Get up each day before the sunrise and see how your life changes. Most people come home from work and are tired. On the weekends they wish to relax. These are luxuries you receive once you've made it. There is always going to be someone who wants what you have, if you relax too much, they'll catch up to you. Don't wait for opportunities to come to you, create them for yourself. Every day you wake up, prepare to grind.

172. **Success occurs when your dreams get bigger than your excuses** ~ Excuses are bountiful; they'll always be there for you. We make excuses for why we can't do something or why we can't live the life we wish. When is enough going to be enough? Are you going to rise above your excuses? We all don't feel like working sometimes, but those who are successful push through it. With your elaborate dreams, do you think you'll be able to work like the average person and be able to attain them? Sacrifice your time now; it's going to pay dividends in the future.

173. **I never worked for the money, only the freedom** ~ Chasing the money will only lead you so far. Chasing the freedom, however—that's another story. Freedom to do what you want with your life. Freedom to show up when you want. Freedom to take a vacation. Freedom to make as much money as you wish. Freedom to attend your children's events. That's what freedom is. Money is a circumstance of that freedom, but it isn't the whole part. If you're working on making an impact each day, your life will become more fulfilling. Wouldn't it be nice to love what you're doing while also not having to worry about the money?

174. **Each morning we are born again. What we do today matters most** ~ We can be so focused on the past and future that we forget the present. We have an average of 70,000 thoughts per day. Why wouldn't you want those thoughts to be focused on what you're doing in the moment? Block off the distractions that aren't going to get you to where you want to go. Compile a list of tasks you need to do today that's going to give you a better tomorrow. Don't focus on what you need to do tomorrow, only today. Each day is the fresh start of a new life. Will you take advantage of it?

175. **Think about your legacy. You're writing it every day** ~ Every waking moment of your day you are consciously or unconsciously working on your future. And your future will be determined by the work you get done today, not next week or next year. You need to be living in the present but with the foresight that what you do every day will be your future. You need to know that, the moment you die, you will leave your life's work behind—and then what will you be remembered for? For nothing? For greatness? It's up to you. Wake up each day with a purpose and goals, while getting sh*t done.

176. **Every champion was once a contender who refused to give up** ~ No one starts out as a pro; we're all amateurs at first. How do you get better? By putting yourself in uncomfortable positions. This might be someone who is tougher or more skilled than you. You have to work yourself through the ranks to get to the top. You're going to have to fight battles against yourself and against others. Come prepared to every fight or else you're going to get knocked out. You are going to have to outwork the other guy. You can't see him, but if you sit idle long enough, he'll appear right before your eyes.

177. **I want to inspire people. I want someone to look at me and say because of you, I didn't give up** ~ My goal isn't to live forever, it's to create something that will. I believe that every day when we wake up, we have two options: Pursue success or follow the path to nowhere. For the longest time in my life, I didn't do anything. I wasn't getting better in any area of my life. It's when I finally said that I had enough that I started to take my life seriously. There have been struggles and failures, but the taste of success trumps it all. You're going to have to put your head down and get at it. No one is going to discipline you, you have to do it for yourself. No one is going to tell you to work, you have to do it.

178. **A winner is just a loser who tried one more time** ~ Legends don't become legends by staying in their comfort zone. They become legends, joining the 'Greats' by continuously pushing through society's norms while paving their own path in life. Never be afraid of failing. In fact, failing a lot at the beginning is the shortcut toward success. Keep moving forward, try new things, face the absolute toughest competitors and keep training your craft because the more you face people better than you, the better you will become. And you just might become the world champion—as long as you never give up.

179. **Have confidence in yourself and what you believe in even if people think you're crazy** ~ People are going to think you're crazy whether you do or don't go after your dreams. People might laugh at you for your high ambitions, but they'll back off when you start to become successful. No idea is too crazy or too big. Have the conviction to know what you're doing is going to change the world. Even if it doesn't change the world and only affects a few people, that's exceptional. Most people go their entire life without making an impact. That's not you. You were put here to make an impact.

180. **If you say you can't pursue your dreams because you don't have enough money, you're making excuses** ~ Why do you think you need to have money to create an impact on this world? I started my first business with $75, a dream and a hustle. Not having enough money is a limitation you put on yourself. There's tons of businesses that you can start for next to nothing; a blog, drop shipping, creating a valuable online product—the options are endless. Don't let money hold you back from chasing your dreams. When you set out to make an impact, the money will soon follow. Steve Jobs was never focused on making money, he was focused on changing the world. Don't be in it for the money, be in it to help as many people as possible.

181. **Motivation? It's easy, just remind yourself that your dreams aren't going to build themselves** ~ This is by far the best way to stay motivated. You can have a brilliant idea, but it never gets to the marketplace. Why is that? Because you didn't execute. Coming up with an idea isn't the hard part. Implementing your idea is where it gets hard. No one will tell you to get up early. No one will tell you that you have to work long hours in the beginning. These are traits that you have to develop on your own. No one is ever going to hand you success, you have to go out there on your own and get it.

182. **At first they'll ask why you're doing it, later they'll ask how you did it** ~ In the beginning, everyone around you is going to question you. People aren't going to see what you see. I saw an opportunity to get out of the middle class and live my dreams. With each step you make, you'll only get questioned more. Everyone suddenly becomes an expert. Sometimes they make you question yourself. Remember, you were put on this path for a reason. If it doesn't work out the first time, you can always pick yourself up and try again. One day you're going to stand as a champion and everyone is going to ask you how you did it.

183. **One year from now, you'll wish you started today** ~ Why are you waiting until tomorrow? Tomorrow becomes next week, next month, and next year. The longer you put off your dreams, the quicker someone else is going to achieve them. You have a finite amount of time in this world. You can waste it or you can create something that's going to give you a lasting legacy. Do you really want to wake up every day, slogging through something you hate? Your life doesn't have to be this way. There are tons of examples of people out there who have become successful and didn't have an easy past. Rise above all excuses you make for yourself and start today.

184. **We don't grow when things are easy, we grow when we face challenges** ~ You're going to face challenges over and over again. With each challenge, you can either back down or push through. Your lack of money is a great challenge to overcome. Not having any resources is an excellent challenge to overcome. The world will try and knock you down, but you aren't going to let that happen. You're going to develop a toughness that's unique. You're going to laugh at challenges, you're going to wish you had to go through tougher ones because they're too easy to overcome. When you find yourself at this point, you're on the fast track for success.

185. **When you have a mission, you don't sleep until it's complete** ~ Do you know what it really takes to be successful? It's sacrificing yourself every day for the greater good. It's not f*cking easy becoming successful, but it can be done. It's going to take massive amounts of effort. You're going to have to show radical differences in every aspect of your life. The only way your business is going to grow is if you grow. If you don't like the situation you're in, you can change it! No one is holding you back except yourself. Do whatever it takes to become successful.

186. **I'm not ignoring you, I'm plotting my next million** ~ Your time is very valuable, it shouldn't be wasted on non-sense activities. If you let others dictate your life, you'll eventually run out of time. You can never get your time back. I wish you could see how much time you have left because then you wouldn't waste it. The successful and unsuccessful each have 24 hours. How you use yours is going to determine the life you live. Manage your time well: Create a schedule and do whatever it takes so you don't lose your time. Have your commitments, not your emotions dictate your behavior. With each activity you partake in, make sure you're spending your time wisely.

187. **Haters only see the public glories, never the private sacrifices** ~ You get praised in the light for what you do in the dark. No one is going to see you working weekends or getting up early in the morning. They believe you work the same as everyone else. This is why we're in awe when we see someone who's successful: We don't understand how it's possible. People tend to think that success comes easy or that it happens overnight, but this couldn't be further from the truth. Especially in the beginning, you're going to have to grind whether you feel like it or not. You're not going to know if your idea is going to work. Overcome this fear by taking action. Over time, everything will come together and the pieces will click. It's going to be the most rewarding journey.

188. **Being rich isn't a goal. $100,000 per month is a goal** ~ A goal and a wish are not the same thing. A wish is a hopeful thought, a goal is a vision that has a timeline on which you are working towards every day. It's time to forget wishes and bullsh*t goals. The next goal you make, make it for 90 days and then make monthly, weekly and daily mini-goals. By completing them every day, you will destroy your main goal. That's how Lions do it, and you are in the process of becoming one of the few Lions in a world populated by sheep.

189. **A true Lion lives life on his own terms** ~ A true Lion doesn't let others dictate his life. A true Lion goes after what he wants despite what the naysayers say. He intends to live the best he can. He's the top in his industry, with the gorgeous wife and beautiful house. No matter what you do, he will always be on top. He's playing chess while you're playing checkers. A true Lion sacrifices himself for the greater good of his family. Are you ready to become a true Lion?

190. **Every woman deserves a man who will proudly praise her in front of other women, not the one who praises other women in front of her** ~ When you are single, have fun, a blast and do as you like but, once you have committed yourself to a relationship with another person, you keep your eyes on them. That doesn't mean you don't find others sexy or attractive, because you will. But being with someone means you have enough self-worth and appreciation of your significant other to keep it to yourself. Let's bring back chivalry, let your woman or your man know that you love them, believe in them and are their biggest fan in public and private.

191. **Pay close attention to those who don't clap when you win** ~ Sometimes those closest around you will want to see your empire fall. They get jealous and they can only feel better by putting you down. They may act like they're there for you, but it's not true. Pay close attention to those who share in your success. Do they hang around you because you're successful or because they actually like you? Only time will tell who a true person is. Be careful who you share your words with, it may come back to haunt you.

192. **There's only one way to success, it's called hard work** ~ People are always asking the secret to success, as if there's some magic fairy dust you can buy that's going to make you millions overnight. Well, guess what, that's never going to f*cking happen. Even the people who win the lottery go broke within a couple of years. You have to build an empire from the ground up, brick by brick. People don't want to tell you the sacrifices you're going to have to make. You're going to have to do sh*t you don't want to do. You're going to have to live below your means for years to come—and success is never guaranteed.

193. **Beware of vision, dream, and passion killers, and if you see them, f*ck them and keep working** ~ There are always going to be negative people trying to knock you down and keep you down. They do this because they are losers. They do this because they have nothing going for them or, if they do, they are not on your level. They do this because they are insecure with themselves and their position in life. Knowing this, stay away from them. The moment you realize someone is like this, leave them behind. In the game of success, there are already enough problems, so there is no need to bring losers and dream killers into the picture.

194. **97% of the people who give up are employed by the 3% who never gave up** ~ Do you want to be one of those people who give up? Or are you going to be among the 3% who never gave in? When everything was against them, they pushed through. They went through life's toughest challenges, but came out the other side. If you look at the employees in the world, the majority of them gave up on their dreams. Do you wish to have someone giving you orders? Wouldn't it be nice to have it the other way around? The greatest risk you can take is that you think you're going to be okay by working for someone else. They can let you go at any moment. The best part about being an entrepreneur? You can never get fired.

195. **A great future doesn't require a great past** ~ You could have had a great past or a terrible one, but that's irrelevant to your future successes. Don't let setbacks, problems and barriers get in your f*cking way. Today is a new day. That goes for a great past, too—do not live on yesterday's successes. If you want to reach the top in your industry, every day you need to wake up and be hungry for more. Every day you wake up, you have a choice to be a Lion or a sheep. Lions don't complain about the situation, they push through it; a Lion also doesn't become 'comfortable.' They always want more and to become more.

196. **Reading is like having conversations with the greatest men who ever lived** ~ There is no reason not to be successful in this life. You can be born into poverty, without mentors, and in a bad place. You may 'think' you can't get out and may 'think' you lack the resources to be successful. However, you all have access to books. Every successful person makes it a priority to read about the people at the top. They study them, learn from them, and then become one themselves. Make it a goal of yours to read at least two books a month and, if you 'can't find the time,' make it.

197. **Nothing is more dangerous than a man who is focused and on a mission** ~ You will not find a more dangerous man than someone who knows where he is going in life. No matter what you do or what you say to him, he can't be stopped. He doesn't care what gets in his way, he's going to become successful. He never wants to be like the others, living a mediocre life. He understands that he was put on this planet to make a difference. He's the man we all look up to, the one who's at the top in his industry. People can hate on him as much as they want, but it doesn't faze him. It's time you start becoming him.

198. **Remember, those who said you couldn't do it are watching** ~ There will be multiple instances in your life where people doubt you. People will tell you time and time again that you can't do something because they can't do it themselves. Just because it's too hard for them doesn't mean you can't do it. I used to put up my own barriers, telling myself that I couldn't do something because of other people's opinion about me. It took years to overcome my limitations. What makes it easy is if you use the doubt that people throw onto you as motivation. Be constantly pushing yourself. It's time you prove the doubters wrong.

199. **A true Lion doesn't need a crowd to boost his ego** ~ When you are an alpha in life, whether a man or woman, you do not need the validation of others. Alpha is something that you innately possess. Nobody can narrow it down to a certain trait; it is something you fully embody. You don't focus your energy on your 'followers' or the need to be around the 'popular.' You know you are great and your time is coming when it will unfold. You let others talk about your success, you are mysterious in your work. Lions walk alone or with a few other men or women who have similar goals in life. They need not flock like the many people in our generation. Stop being reliant on others' opinion of you and make your own perception of yourself, the only one that is real.

200. **It's going to happen because I'm going to make it happen** ~ Go into anything in life with the attitude that you can and will accomplish it. We have these perceived battles already in us. We know what we should be doing, but most of the time we don't do it. People know that smoking or eating fatty foods isn't good for you, yet they still do it. You have control over every thought. If you think you're about to make a decision you're going to regret, walk away. It's as simple as that. Once you start to believe in yourself, you become unstoppable.

201. **I want a relationship where people know of us, but nothing about us** ~ When you are successful in life, people will know, based on the way you act, dress, and hold yourself everywhere you go. But them knowing you are successful is different from them knowing everything you do or how you got there. Be mysterious. It's much more interesting and alluring to the masses. You and your partner should always go after the riches in life, both in wealth and experiences, but there is no need to post every little thing you do. Be that couple that many see from afar, but can't quite say any specifics about. And if you do it that way, you will become irresistible to people because of the mystery you two share—and of course, you both need to become successful first, for this to happen.

202. **Everyone wants to eat, but few are willing to hunt** ~ Everyone wants to have the luxurious house, sports car, and trophy wife, but not everyone is willing to put in the work. I've always been one to judge more by results than by words spoken. You can talk about all that you're going to accomplish, even about the life you're going to have. The difference between the successful and the unsuccessful is that the successful back those words up. They understand that it might not happen as quickly as they like, but they prefer delayed gratification. Put in the work now and be thinking long term.

203. **Be the architect of your future, not a prisoner of your past** ~ Stop living in your past, whether it was great or terrible. You can't live off past accomplishments or failures. The only thing that counts today is what you do today and your plans for the future. You can be anything you want to be and do whatever you want to do, but you absolutely need to leave the victim mentality behind. There's no room for complaining and wishing, only hard work every day towards your vision. You control your future, whether that's Greatness or mediocrity. The choice is yours, and you are a Lion or a Lion in the making, so make the rest of your life the best of your life.

204. **Be the type of man you'd want your daughter to be with** ~ Why not treat a girl with the utmost respect? How you treat your wife is going to have a direct effect on how your daughter views the men of the world. Would you want your daughter dating someone like you? Would you feel comfortable with that? You have the power to choose what type of man you want to be around women and you're constantly setting an example. A true gentleman is always looking for his daughter's best interest. Even if he is divorced, he's not going around and hooking up. He takes his time engaging in conversation. He doesn't lie, even when a truth is hard to tell. Take a real good look at yourself in the mirror. Are you being the best possible man that you can be?

205. **Dear haters, I have so much more for you to be mad at. Just be patient** ~ I would say that there isn't one super successful person in the world that has no haters. Haters, losers and negative people are a part of life. It's inevitable. But we, as successful individuals, can choose how to deal with them, and you should choose: not to deal with them. Who cares what they say? Every time your name comes out of their mouth it's free publicity. And, newsflash, haters, we are Lions and we will have many, many more major successes in our lives that you can hate about with your loser friends. It's that simple. Let the haters hate, and you just focus on being successful.

206. **Never forget those who have been with you from the start** ~ There are two types of people at the beginning of your future successes: Those who support and motivate you and those who are negative and pessimists about you and life in general. This post is about those who supported you when all you had was an idea. They were there from the start. They remember your struggle; they never wavered from their belief in your future successes. Never forget these people, especially when you are a major success. They are the most loyal of your friends and family, while most of your friends and distant relatives now may just be attracted to your present money and power, but were nowhere to be found during your grind to the top. Never forget.

207. **Stop telling people more than they need to know** ~ Only the fool reveals all that they know. Fools love parading around with their seemingly infinite knowledge. They are always open to explaining everything and anything. They tell their secrets, habits, tricks and even how much they have in their bank account. Do not be like this. The predators at the top will gladly take all of your knowledge and, when you have nothing else of value, they'll leave you on the sidewalk. The key is to always say less than you know. Never talk about where you learned something of importance, or any tricks you have up your sleeve. Let your actions speak for you. Be quiet, be strategic, and observe the crowd. Try to pry information out of others, especially competitors, without talking about yourself or your ways. And remember, everyone loves to talk about themselves, except those that understand this power move.

208. **I did not come to this world to be average** ~ Why would you ever want to live a life of mediocrity? A life where you have an average wife, an average house, or even an average car? I've always been one to want more for myself and what I'm doing. I don't play small. Develop an abundance mindset and understand that there's plenty to go around, that nothing can stop you on your path to greatness. You only have one life, why would you ever want to go small?

209. **My success isn't a result of arrogance, it's a result of belief** ~ People will call you arrogant when you express belief in yourself. But you have to believe in yourself if you want to be successful! There will be people who doubt you time and time again. It's up to you to prove them wrong. Don't keep b*tching that he or she is cocky if they can back it up. Only small minds will run away in fear. Surround yourself with those who are going to lift you up and you'll start to see an amazing transformation in your life. Don't be afraid of becoming great and spreading your words.

210. **Just because it's the weekend doesn't mean you stop grinding** ~ During the grind stage of your life, days off are for losers. Bill Gates never took a day off in his 20s, and look where he is today. The people who preach that days off are 'healthy' are right, but they will not get the results that people who say, 'Screw it, I am going to work like hell' are going to get... People who are putting in hours every day are uncommon people. People who are sacrificing temporary pleasure for eternal greatness. They are life's game changers. Be someone who works regardless of the day: Sunday, holiday, etc. If you want to live your dream, you need to be working harder and smarter than your competition. Do not lose focus and surround yourself with other Lions that are waking up early and getting things done on the weekend.

211. **Create a life you don't need a vacation from** ~ If you love Fridays more than Mondays, it's time to rethink your career. Don't stop pursuing your passion until you have found it. It could take months, years, even a decade or two to find out what you're passionate about. This isn't wasted time. Millions, if not billions of people go their entire lives and never find their passion. Find a way to monetize what you're doing and you'll never work a day in your life. You might not find your passion right away, but that doesn't mean you should give up. I wrote an entire fiction novel before I realized I love writing about entrepreneurship and self-development more. Each step of the journey will lead you to where you want to go.

212. **I do have an unfair advantage over you. I don't quit. Ever** ~ This is how you get ahead of everyone else. In a society where people need safe spaces, they're going to give up at the first sign of danger. When your back is against the wall, are you going to give up? If you quit, you have to start all over again. Wouldn't it be easier to make the business you're in right now work? You have the knowledge within you to become successful, you just have to use it. Difficult circumstances are there to test you. You start a clothing line and all the shirts are too small and you can't get a refund and you have to figure out what to do next. That's an example of difficulty that could arise on your journey. Do you have the power to overcome it?

213. **Do not try to fight a Lion if you aren't one yourself** ~ One way to lose for sure is to go against someone who is a Lion and you are but a sheep or a Lion in progress. Failure is inevitable. Humiliation and regret should be expected. If you are not yet a Lion, you must be working daily to become one. Study the sh*t out of your daily habits and see where you are making progress and where you are lacking and then have the self-discipline to change where change is necessary to Become The Lion. And once you are a Lion, your opponents will respect and fear you as an adversary.

214. **I'm not here to fit in your world. I'm here to make my own** ~ Why would you ever want to live by society's rules? It sure sounds fun living a job you hate for 40 years and if you happen to make it out alive, you can travel the world, but guess what? You can't walk. Why not create a life that enables you to do what you want all year round? There are millions of people who are doing that in this exact moment. They're no different than you or me. They said to hell with society's standards, I'm setting sail on my own boat and do you know what? Those people haven't looked back since.

215. **What you teach your son, you teach your son's son** ~ It's not just about your children. When you teach your children and mentor them, you are in essence, influencing their children and whoever they run into in life, which is why it's so important to take your job as a parent seriously. But, in order to teach your children the right way, you must become a person of character and knowledge. And that only comes from conscious effort that you put in every day on becoming a better person. You cannot teach someone something you have no idea about or haven't done. Why? Because you look like a phony and no one will take you seriously. So start with yourself, become a Lion in your own life and then teach others.

216. **A man's money will never excite an independent woman** ~ Women and men alike are looking for a partner who is financially stable. When you are not financially stable, it takes a toll on your relationship, so make it a priority to take care of yourself first, before you commit to another person. That being said, when you are a person of independence, you should not go after someone simply because they are rich. By doing that, you are showing your true colors. You should like the person for who they are and what they are about. You should be attracted to their plans for the future and what they want out of life, not their bank account. If you are a person of riches, keep it quiet, and find a person who is right for you without bringing money into it. And then, once you get to know them, you can open up.

217. **If you want to be successful you have to be willing to disappear for a while** ~ My friends and family used to question where I was. They would say things like, "We never see you anymore" or "You've disappeared." Do you know what this means? It means you're putting in the grind! You're going to have to hide away and put in the work. If everyone knows where you are at every single moment of the day, how are you supposed to get work done? Work diligently and silently, creating a fireworks show along the way. Keep everyone on their toes and guessing what you're going to do next.

218. **When achieving your goal is more important than partying, welcome to the 1% club** ~ Are you thinking about the weekend or how you're going to continue to grind to get all of your goals done? If you want to be a part of the 1% club, you're not partying. You party once you get to be successful, not during the process. You have to be willing to work while others are partying, sleeping, even eating. There is so much time to be had, but it may not feel like a lot to you because you keep wasting it and for what reason? It's time you start taking your life serious.

219. **Hurt me with a truth but never comfort me with a lie** ~ When you are a person of character, you can handle criticism. The only people that cannot, and would rather be lied to, are the insecure. This is a fact. Criticism is a part of life and it's a big part of the successful life. It's how people can reach the top. The people at the bottom and the middle do not want to hear how they can improve or what they are doing wrong. Be a winner, a Lion: Ask for and accept criticism.

220. **The secret to success: You have to want it more than the other person and be willing to die for it** ~ Only those who go too far can truly understand how far they can go. There are countless stories of entrepreneurs who failed time and time again, but they didn't let that get them down. They picked themselves up and kept trying. They had one option, to succeed! You can go from being broke to being a millionaire. You can go from being a millionaire to being broke if you relax and think you're all set. Try going for a one-mile run every single day for a year or read 30 books in a month. This is how you gain confidence to succeed. You push yourself beyond the limit of what you think is possible.

221. **Treat me like a King and I'll treat you like a Queen. Treat me like a game and I'll show you how it's played** ~ A lot of people are not serious when it comes to relationships. They would rather sleep around, be single, and have fun. And, if that's what you are dealing with, play the game. Don't try and try again if the person you like wants to be single and have fun. That is the worst. Accept their stance, and find someone else that you can call your King or Queen. Someone who will love and be with you and only you. That being said, have fun yourself during your early years and, once you are in a relationship, be committed.

222. **It's only after we've lost everything that we're free to do anything** ~ Sometimes in life, you lose everything. Your business fails, you breakup with your significant other and you're devastated. Instead of looking at this in a negative light, understand that this is your fresh start. A start to find someone who's more amazing than the person you just were with. You can take your newfound knowledge from your past business and employ it into your new venture. Sometimes losing everything is a blessing, not a curse; it all depends on how you look at it.

223. **Those at the top of the kingdom never got there by following the crowd** ~ Everyone at one point or another started from the bottom. The majority who have been successful were never handed it, they had to bust their asses every day to make it happen! When others were sleeping, they were grinding. When others were partying, they were grinding. If you haven't noticed yet, the successful are not your average people nor do they care to be. They lay it all out on the line, all of the time. They aren't afraid of taking risks and just get the job done. It's time you start showing them some respect.

224. **If you're the smartest person in the room, you're in the wrong room** ~ Everyone has heard this advice at some point in their life, but have you put it to work? Who you surround yourself with is who you will become. When you hang out with life's losers and people of a 'victim' mindset, you will become one. It's that simple... That being said, are you the smartest or most successful person in your group? Well then it's your job to find a new group, people who you can learn from and are better than you so that you are always moving forward in life. Re-evaluate your crew and start taking action.

225. **Your life is your business, don't let someone else run it** ~ People have others run their life. It could be through telling them what to do at work and even what to wear because they are on autopilot. They don't think or even speak up for themselves. This is your life. No one should be telling you what you can and can't do. It's time you start taking charge and becoming responsible for your actions. If you don't like something speak up. Quit being a little b*tch all the time and moaning that life isn't fair. We all have to go through it—it's time you grow up!

226. **Money is not the problem; your poor mentality is** ~ Your thinking is either going to make you or break you. You keep making excuses as to why you won't become successful, when in reality we all have the odds stacked against us. Whoever told you that it was going to be easy? You made that lie up in your head. It was never going to be easy; you have push through any pain that might come your way because, believe me, it's going to happen. Push yourself further than what you thought was possible. If you think you can only save 5% of your paycheck, try 10%. Being comfortable at being uncomfortable.

227. **They never thought I would get this far; they were right, I got even further** ~ I remember not getting accepted to all the colleges my friends got into. I had lower S.A.T. scores. The system told me I wasn't ready for college. They told me I'd be an employee my entire life. They told me to stop following my dreams and to not think big. At every major point in my life they were there to predict I'd fail. Every time they told me to stop doing something, I'd use that as motivation to push myself further. I'd been doubted my entire life. Now those who doubted me wonder as to how I've gone so far. What they don't realize is that only your opinion of yourself matters. And my opinion was that I'm going to do whatever it takes to become successful.

228. **A relationship with no arguments is a relationship of many secrets** ~ No relationship is perfect. None. But that is where the beauty lies. Whenever there's an argument, there is room for growth. And that growth is necessary to become the strongest couple you can possibly become. Couples with no arguments are hiding something. That being said, do not go out looking for disagreements—but do know that, when they come, it is an opportunity to move forward and become that much stronger than you were before.

229. **The Devil whispers "Be afraid of the storm." The warrior responds, "I am the storm"** ~ You have one life and you can either live it like a warrior or like a peasant. A peasant always needs to be told what to do, what direction to go in and what to believe in, while warriors pave their own path. They make their own moves and they follow their own vision. Warriors don't complain or b*tch about their situation, no matter what it is; they take their situation and choke it into submission. Be a warrior. Accept responsibility for where you are in life and have the courage to go hard in the direction of your ultimate vision, no matter what 'they' say.

230. **Forget yesterday. Stop saying tomorrow. Let's kill it today** ~ Why focus on the past and future when you're living in the present? Don't think about what you have to do tomorrow or what you didn't do yesterday—focus on today. Focus on your success list for today and today only. If you continue to live in the future, you're not going to get anything done. If you live in the future, you're doomed to repeat your mistakes. Your better tomorrow depends entirely on what you do today. Take a step forward each day, even if it's small.

231. **Cut the bullshit. If you don't find that reason why your dreams are worth more than anything else, you will find yourself doing anything else** ~ You need to have a clear vision for where you want to be in life and never lose sight of it. But it's not enough to have a vision; you must make that vision your number one priority. You need to be working on it every day and never become content. The people who have all the time in the world to fool around and are always free to do anything are people with no goals or a vision. Don't be like them. Set priorities in your life and establish a block of time at the same time every day to work on making your vision reality.

232. **Winners focus on winning. Losers focus on winners** ~ You need to focus on yourself, your mission, and your life. People become sidetracked by following too many people on social media and feel the need to know everything about their lives. But the truth is that you should follow only a few key people, the true legends, and forget the rest. You require too much attention to spread yourself out. Whatever your industry, you need to learn and study that industry so that you can learn everything about it. You then need to plan out how you will reach the top. And then have the guts to stick it out when times are tough and that will require your total focus.

233. **Cheers to all the people working on their vision and not working for the weekend** ~ The start of the weekend for most people is a time to forget about the week's hard work and rejoice over two days of off time—but I bet that is not you. A Lion celebrates when they actually accomplish something, not just because they survived the first five days of the week. That is a sheep's mindset. Make a promise to yourself that you will delay gratification until you are successful, or have accomplished something worth celebrating. Work hard this weekend and leave nothing on the table.

234. **Love her as if there's someone working 24 hours to take her from you** ~ When you find that girl who's going to support you in everything you do, don't let her go. It doesn't matter if you have different interests. What matters is that you continually work every day to push each other and make each other better. A true gentleman courts his woman more than just one night, he does it every day. He understands that it's the simple actions that matter the most. Don't stop searching until you find the one for you. Yes, you may go through some hard times, but having her by your side will make it much easier.

235. **A real friend accepts you for who you are, but helps you become who you should be** ~ A real friend will always accept you for who you are, but will continually help you become the legend you were born to be. When you find this type of friend, keep them, they are too rare to be treated like everyone else. And you also should always be looking out for your friends. Tell them and show them how they could be so much more, if only they tweaked some habits and their mindset. And that goes both ways, take your friends' criticism and feedback and use it. These friends are not a dime a dozen; they are super rare and they want you to succeed and reach your highest potential.

236. **Some people will never like me and I will never give a f*ck** ~ Most people do not like those who are ambitious. They do not like those who have massive goals and an ultimate vision. And they especially do not like those who are working on their goals every day and are committed. They don't like them because they don't understand them. They don't like them because they do not have the self-discipline and ambition themselves to go after their own goals—if they even have any. And you know what: Who gives a f*ck what they think? Seriously. If you want to become the strongest version of yourself and become the absolute top in your industry, you can't please everyone. And who would want to, anyway? Accept your individuality and, if someone doesn't like it, f*ck it. This is your life. Make your own moves and live your ultimate vision without a care about what 'they' would say or think about it.

237. **When you live your life by poor standards you inflict damage on everyone who crosses your path** ~ Do you ever think about how you're going to feel after you spend a night drinking? When you're hungover, there are people who are chasing their dreams. You can barely function the entire day. You're pissing your night away trying to hook up with a girl who's not going to be in alignment with your dreams. The girl you're looking to be your life partner isn't going to be found at a bar. And then—here comes Monday and you hate your job and life. You wonder why? It's because the poor choices you make every day add up over time. You might give in every now and then not realize what it's going to do to your life. When you hang out with people who aren't going anywhere in their life, do you want to be like them? A true Lion sets the highest standards for themselves and then exceeds them.

238. **Fall in love with the process and the results will come** ~ You can follow your passion or you can follow the money. Let me tell you, passion is always going to win. When times get tough and you're following the money, you're going to give up. 85% of all people hate their jobs, yet they're okay with them. If you want to get ahead in life you have to be willing to take chances. I'd rather grind every single day than work a few hours a week doing something I hate. Find something that's going to make you stay up late and get you out of bed early in the morning. Don't stop until you find your calling.

239. **You have unlimited potential. Just because someone doesn't see it, doesn't mean it's not there. Trust your vision and go after it** ~ Many people will never see, understand, or believe in what you are doing and that is great. Why? Because you do not need the support of negative, short-sighted people in your quest to fulfill your ultimate vision. The only thing you need is you. You need to believe in yourself, but more than that, you must have the work ethic and hunger to accomplish great things and live a legendary life! It's not going to be easy. It's going to be hard as hell, but this is your life and you are the creator. Don't mess it up by following what the masses think. Stick to this formula: Develop a vision for yourself—make milestone goals to reach it (yearly, monthly, weekly, and daily) and never give up.

240. **One week they love me, next week they hate me, both weeks I get paid** ~ For all the people who hate on what you're trying to accomplish, share this statement with them. With passive income, your bank account is constantly going to be growing while you're sleeping. In the seconds they took to think about how much they hate you, you made a sale. View these people as motivation. There was a reason why they gave up on their dreams and want you to give up on yours as well. People can hate on you all they want, but that doesn't change the situation you're in and where you're going.

241. **Do not judge my story based on the chapter you walked in** ~ Every single person you meet has a story. They all have family, friends, problems and achievements. The fact is you should never judge a person based on who they are or what they are doing at the present moment until you get to know them. Many, many of us are in the lost identity phase, not knowing what to do or who we are as a person. Some of us are in the grind stage, and just a few are at the level that everyone wants to be: massive success. The moral is: Don't judge people, for in a few years they could be completely different. A loser could become powerful and a powerful person could become a loser. Respect everyone while focusing on yourself and keep focus on your priorities.

242. **Focus on what you want to become, not where you are today** ~ The person you are today has no bearing on the person you can become in the future, whether that is a legend or a loser. Your past has made you the person you are today, so ask yourself: Is the person you are today the person you ultimately want to be? The answer should always be no. Why? Because you should always be progressing in your one life. Focus on the man or woman you want to be, the legend you have always dreamed of, and then work to make it your reality. Write down the persona, habits, and lifestyle of your ideal self and work toward it every day, becoming the strongest version of yourself through consistency and milestone goals. This is the way of the legend. This is the way of the Lion.

243. **Make more moves and fewer announcements** ~ People are always talking about what they're going to do, but how many times does that goal actually get accomplished? I've always been one to believe that results speak louder than words. You make an announcement once you have hit your goal at hand, not before, telling everyone what you're going to do. I can tell you I want to own a Boeing 757, but it means nothing if I don't put in the work. If you put in the work today, the results will come tomorrow. It's not instant gratification and you're not going to like doing the work 100% of the time. But if you stick with it, you can have anything you want in this world.

244. **An entrepreneur is an investor in self-education** ~ Being an entrepreneur is not easy. An entrepreneur is someone who is in control of their life, whether they are doing great or terrible. It's all up to you. To be an entrepreneur of success, you must be learning, always. Learning everything about your industry, yourself, and your company while never losing sight of your ultimate vision. No one is going to tell you when to wake up, go to bed, read this book, or work on your business. This is the toughest job out there. You call the shots, and you make your own moves, whether they are good or bad. But the rewards? Massive success and a lifestyle of freedom. Just never give up and keep to your vision, no matter how hard it is right now.

245. **Great men are not born great, they grow great** ~ No one becomes famous or successful right away. That person grinds for years at a time to get that way. They understand that they're going to have to overcome limitations and self-doubt that comes their way. Going after your dream is f*cking scary. But do you know what's also scary? Working for someone else and doing something you hate for 40 years. This is your life, so you have to be the one to step up in the face of adversity.

246. **Once you realize what you're worth, nothing can stop you** ~ You set your own self-worth. Anyone who tells you how much you're worth doesn't have any business being in your life. If you ask, you shall receive. If you think you're capable of making $10 an hour, you will; if you think $100 or $1000, you'll get it. It's about understanding what you're worth and knowing that you can get it. Don't let other people tell you your value, show them what you can do. Show them who's boss. You deserve to be the best and you should accept nothing less. Stop putting yourself down to make others feel good. It's time you start acting like a Lion.

247. **The goal isn't to be liked, it's to be respected** ~ Not everyone is going to like you, that's a simple fact of life. You can't please everyone, it's impossible. You'll get criticized for what you do and for what you don't do. I don't care if you don't like me, all I care about is respect. You may not like the other person, but you have to respect them for what they're doing. Because at the end of the day, we all have the same goal; to live life on our own terms. We're not going to get out alive so there's no point in having resentment. Hating someone else takes too much energy. Take that enemy and turn him into an ally. Earn people's respect and you're on your way to the top.

248. **You'll never influence the world by trying to be like it** ~ Most people are average, but I know that if you're reading this book you're not average. Most people work 9-5 for 40 years and call it a life. You influence the world by being different, by doing something only the 1% does. You influence others by helping and uplifting them, or even donating to their cause. You weren't put here to be another cog in the machine; you're much more than that. At the end of the day, it's all about the legacy that you're going to be leaving. Are people going to remember your name for generations?

249. **Move in silence. Never let them know your next move** ~ Only the fool lets everyone know their next move in life. Be private. Whether you like it or not, people, even the ones you least suspect, want what you have... especially if you are successful. As you climb the ladder of success, you are going to need to shield your intentions and your plans. Why? Because they are your plans. You will make them happen and you do not need someone else trying to stop you from going after it or, worse, them taking it from you. Besides, people respect and look up to people who make things happen, rather than what the masses do: just talk and talk about what they are going to do. Be a legend and take action. Let your results speak for who you and what you're about.

250. **You haven't seen a Lamborghini commercial because the people who can afford them aren't sitting and watching TV** ~ It's time to stop whatever you are doing if you are not successful and take account of your habits, lifestyle and priorities. I want you to sit down in a room alone and just think, think of who you want to become and then write down a plan outlining how you will get there and then work your plan and review it every day! And that plan definitely does not require you to be watching TV, partying, or fooling around. It's time to get serious. Grind for the next five years and then you will have a lifetime to do whatever you want.... but you must be grinding right now towards your vision... and that requires you to get rid of the loser habits. It's time to get serious.

251. **If you don't like me and still watch everything I do, you are a fan** ~ When you are successful, you are going to have followers, and many of those followers will not like you. They are jealous, negative and are quick to call you an 'overnight success, which is a common phrase spoken by life's losers. I want you to know they are losers and I want you to not be deterred by these types of people, but instead, use them to motivate you. How? In tough times, think of your haters and use that to spark your fire to accomplish even more in this life. Just never be complacent. Never be comfortable and never care what 'they' say or think.

252. **If you are willing to risk the usual, you will have to settle for the ordinary** ~ I get it, I do. You don't want to take risks. That's perfectly okay; you can work for me, building my dreams. More than likely, you'll hate the commute I give you, the pay you get and even the hours you work. You'll talk about me behind my back, while I continue to accumulate more and more success. If you don't want to hate your life, then start taking some risks. Create affirmations for yourself and read them multiple times per day. Assure yourself that you have what it takes to be successful. There is nothing in the world that can't be accomplished. There are books written on practically everything; when's the last time you read one? Today marks the start of the new grind, so make sure to destroy your goals.

253. **A strong vision is bigger than your excuses** ~ If you create a vision that's large and powerful, you can't have excuses. If you're just trying to adapt and survive, you're going to live a life of mediocrity. How badly do you want it? Because you're going to have to work harder than you think you have to. When everyone is relaxing, are you going to fall into that same habit? There are tons of high-achievers in this world. Reach out to them and seek advice. They will tell you how they got to where they are and you can use that to your advantage. Your journey doesn't have to be lonely, but it certainly won't happen if you make excuses.

254. **A Lion doesn't concern himself with the opinions of sheep** ~ The only opinions you should take into consideration are yours and those who have achieved what you are going after in life. Anyone else's opinion, especially those of the negative, pessimistic sheep, should never be valued. They have achieved nothing. They have no goals. They have no ambition. So why would you care what they think or say about you—or about anything that comes out of their mouth for that matter? They are life's losers. Focus on yourself and your goals. Focus on your ultimate vision and never let them deter you from going after it. Seek counsel and advice from successful people and you will be successful.

255. **Limits are for those who need them** ~ You are the one who decides how far you go in life. When you were young, people probably told you what you could and couldn't do. Why would you listen to them? You're better than them. If you set a plan and you work on that plan every single day, you will be successful. You can accomplish way more than what you think is possible. Where you are today isn't going to be the same place you are a year today or where you are in a decade. The limits you have right now are going to seem silly in the future. Every day, try one new activity that's going to get you out of your comfort zone.

256. **Respect yourself enough to walk away from anything that no longer serves you, grows you, or makes you happy** ~ People say being selfish is bad; well, it's not. When I say selfish, I mean loving yourself and having the self-respect to say no to habits that are bad for you, people that are bad for you, and things that have no place in your life. It's going to be hard to get rid of these things, especially your old friends that do not have your ambition or mindset, but it's necessary for greatness! Focus on yourself, your family, and the people you choose to have in your life because they force you to be better. You have one life; don't waste it by priding yourself on being the best in mediocre company.

257. **Let your faith roar so loud that you can't hear doubt speak** ~ We all have doubt, but we also have faith. We can believe that we're going to fail or we can believe we're going to succeed. Whatever you manifest in your mind each and every single day, will determine the outcome of your life. Are you thinking about the show you want to watch later or are you thinking about the work that has to get done? You can never have two thoughts at once. You must test all of your strength and determine your own thoughts. In a world full of negativity, you'll stand out by being positive.

258. **Success is the sum of small efforts repeated day in and day out** ~ Success doesn't happen overnight. It rarely ever occurs without hard work and determination. Success comes when you put in the hours when you don't feel like it. When you come home from your 9-5, what are you doing? On the weekends when most are watching football, what are you doing? Understand that you only have one life and every second you let go by is a second that you can't get back. Success is never easy nor will it ever be. When you prepare each and every day, through the dark and good times, you'll have your chance. It might be in the introduction to someone new. Keep improving and don't let up, your breakthrough is coming.

259. **Sometimes your circle decreases in size but increase in value** ~ If you look closely at a successful person, you will notice that they do not have hundreds of friends. They often do not even have over 5 friends... Why? It's not because they are losers. It's not because they don't like people. It's because they value great company and they want to be surrounded by life's game changers.... and those people are rare. So if you find them, keep them and stay in touch... Surround yourself with those who have similar ambition and a vision for the future... and understand the importance of hanging out with only those of a similar path. Find fellow killers in life and build your empires together.

260. **Not everyone deserves to know the real you** ~ You don't have to speak to everyone. Not everyone needs to know everything about you. Let them see your success, they'll call you lucky. They won't see the late nights and early mornings. They won't see the sacrifices or dedications you've made. Let people chastise the person they think you are. Keep them on the outside. Only a select few should know about you and what you do. The less you speak, they better you are. Words can cause problems if you speak too much. Keep your mouth shut and speak only when needed. You'll rise to the top, while everyone else is fighting at the bottom.

261. **You're only one decision away from a totally different life** ~ What's the one thing that you've been putting off? Is it that phone call that you're scared to make? Is it your dream you don't want to go after? Why? Why don't you want to go after what you want in life? There is nothing stopping you. You can b*tch and complain, but you have to be the one to change the circumstance you're in. The next decision you make could be the one that changes your life. It's not easy, nor will it ever be. If it was easy, everyone would be doing it. Start an action plan, step by step. Moving a foot forward is better than sitting on the couch.

262. **It's what we do in life that echoes in eternity** ~ Every waking moment of your day, you are consciously or unconsciously working on your future. And your future will be determined by the work you get done today, not next week or next year. You need to be living in the present but with the foresight that what you do every day will be your future and your ultimate legacy. You need to know that the moment you die, you will leave your life's work behind. And then what will you be remembered for? For nothing? For greatness? It's up to you. Wake up each day on purpose and have goals to fulfill that purpose. And remember, after you die you cannot work on your legacy, so use your time wisely.

263. **F*ck excuses. Learn to admit when you f*ck up** ~ Only the cowards cannot admit when they know they messed up. They do not have the self-confidence to blame themselves, so they continue to blame everything and everybody to avoid the truth. Do not be like them. Lying is a purely sheep thing to do. Lions, however, can fully own up to their mistakes. Why? Because they realize that messing up and failing is the pathway to Greatness. They realize that every mistake is a step forward in the right direction. They look at life as a marathon, not a sprint. Have this mentality. Always believe in yourself and in your vision and have the character to be true to yourself and others.

264. **Learn to fight alone** ~ If you want to reach the top, lead an empire, while becoming the strongest version of yourself, you must be willing to fight alone. Have the self-confidence and character to go after your vision every day, even on the days you don't feel like it. You need to understand that the quantity of people has nothing to do with success. It's all about the quality. Become the strongest version of yourself and you can beat an army of hundreds. Just think of Achilles, the best warrior that ever lived. He marched to his own drum, and you can do the same. Always be learning more than the competition and embrace your struggles towards greatness.

265. **Every genius mind is at least a little bit insane** ~ When you have a great idea and put it into execution, you're going to be called all sorts of names. Don't you think that Thomas Edison was called crazy when he was failing over hundreds of experiments? What do we call him now? Genius. Elon Musk, Steve Jobs, Warren Buffet. All of those guys were called crazy. When you have a vision that's so impactful that you can't sleep at night and it consumes your every thought, that's crazy. But it's good to be crazy. Crazy passionate, crazy about changing the world. People will look down upon you. Don't let someone who's done nothing tell you how to do anything.

266. **Keep friends that do good things behind your back and bad things to your face** ~ People just aren't the same as they were a hundred years ago. People of character are rare while cowards and backstabbers are everywhere. That being said, who you spend your time with is ultimately who you will become. You must be on a continuous search for friends that have character. Find individuals who will motivate you. Individuals who have their own goals in life and who are absolutely comfortable in their own skins. They are not jealous of your success, they pride in it. They will always tell you the truth, good or bad, to your face. But they will never bad-mouth you to another person, because that is not what people of character do. And for yourself, cut the gossip and bullsh*t while focusing on your character.

267. **Some of the greatest people come from the darkest places** ~ Not everyone starts out from a bright place. Some of us have had to overcome circumstances that are unimaginable to most. It doesn't matter where you start off in life, it matters where you finish. You can hit rock bottom, but understand that you can go up. Don't listen to what everyone else is telling you. It's never easy on the journey towards success. You might think of giving up from time to time, but you'll regret it if you do. There is someone out there who is living the life you want to live. Why can't that be you?

268. **Life is such a great teacher that when you don't learn a lesson, it will repeat it** ~ Life is better than any teacher, and the way life teaches is through first-hand experience. Not from reading, not from mentors, but from trial and error. Reading and mentors can catapult you years ahead in the game of success, but you will still need to go out there and experience what you are learning. You need to get out of your comfort zone and be willing to do what others will not. You need to understand that if you do not understand your mistakes, you will make them again, which is why you must be a strategic warrior in life. Analyze your every move and learn from your every mistake. This is the way of the legend. This is the way towards greatness.

269. **Making dad proud has always been the goal** ~ I'm not here to make anyone proud except myself and my family. I don't care what others think. I care what my father thinks, his opinion on the matter. Your family raised you and turned you into the person that you became today. Are you going to show them appreciation? Take time out of every day and let them know how much they mean to you and how grateful you are for them. Without them, your life would be a disaster. They helped guide you through the light and dark times. Be thankful for everything you have. And don't forget them on your road to the top.

270. **If you're not losing friends you're not growing up** ~ I used to be friends with tons of people. My circle has been cut down dramatically. As you grow and reach new levels in your life, you realize that you don't need everyone. Some people you just talked to every day, but nothing more than that. On your journey, you're going to lose friends. Some of them will doubt you and you don't need them in your life. Others you will no longer have time to talk to and the relationship will dissipate. Take this is a sign that you are growing stronger. If you want to be successful, you're going to have to disappear for a while.

271. **When people ask me where I'm going? I say "To the top"** ~ This is the type of confidence you must possess if you are ever going to reach the top. You must believe in yourself fully and never let other people deter you and your vision. That being said, you must not only believe you will reach the top but you must have the work ethic too. And when I say work ethic I mean having a major vision that you break down into yearly, monthly, weekly, and daily goals. You must plan your rise years in advance so that you actually know where you will end up. Why? Because it's hard as hell. Have a structured plan and don't float through life like all the sheep of the world—and remember, the road to the top is the hardest road, but it is worth all the struggle.

272. **Become so financially secure that you forget it's payday** ~ If you are trying to live the best life possible, money should never be an issue. You should be so financially secure that you have multiple streams of income, so that if one business were to fail, it would mean relatively nothing to your empire. That is the power of multiple streams of income. This is the power of the rich, but how do you get there? By an intense hunger to learn about different business models, especially online. Why? Because the Internet has allowed for innumerable ways to make passive income. It just takes a willingness to learn. And, if you are not making passive income right now, read our free book on our site on how to get started.

273. **Stop trying so hard for people who don't even care** ~ I learned early on in life that you can't please everyone, no matter how hard you try. Whatever you do, people will hate you. At the end of the day, you can only please yourself. You're all you have. Stop trying to be perfect, because you never will be. No matter how hard you try, it'll never happen. Do the things that please yourself. I tried being like everyone else and it sucked. Society wants to keep you average; they don't want you to get ahead of everyone else. I can't understand this, but most people live their life like this. Choose to do what makes you happy and go against what society tells you that you should be.

274. **Warriors look at problems as pathways to wisdom and character while losers ask "Why me?"** ~ You can choose to look at your problems as roadblocks or as gateways. Roadblocks end in frustration, procrastination and, worse, you will develop b*tch habits from backing down and this will make it 10 times as easy to fall into this sheep habit again. That is why you must choose to live by the Warrior's code. Warriors do not complain or subside from their mission as problems arise. They go right f*cking through them, for legends, warriors, and people at the top fully realize that every problem is the opportunity to become wiser in their life. They destroy problems at their conception. They break their problem's neck before it has time to grow. This is the way of the warrior.

275. **I'm always loyal to those who are loyal to me** ~ If you're going to say something about me, say it to my face. Be a man. Those who are loyal will tell you what's real. You may not like it in the beginning, but you'll get over it. It doesn't matter if your crew has been with you since the beginning or if you're finding a new one right now. All that matters is that they push you to achieve your dreams. They tell what you can do and where to improve. They help you as much as you can and you help them as much as you can. You understand that you're all in it together.

276. **Don't be upset because you're at the low level of success. Just remember, a cub is still a Lion** ~ Absolutely do not feel bad if you are at the low level of success if you are grinding but, if you are not grinding and you are at the bottom, you should feel bad. You should feel like a loser. Losers do nothing and just complain, while winners have a winning mentality, and that mentality is a decision—a decision to keep going and working every day while ignoring life's sheep. Winners are constantly learning, grinding and studying to get better. But they do fail at times; however, they keep on going. The path towards success is never the easy path. The only objective in your life right now is progress and not making the same mistakes. Learn and adapt your way to success and never feel bad for yourself; just focus on where you are going in life.

277. **Be patient. Everything is coming together** ~We want instant gratification. We want success to be easy and not have to work too hard. We want to not have to take any risks or make sacrifices. We assume that we'll be a millionaire in a month, better yet a week. There's a strong difference between what you want and taking action. Success will never happen overnight. It takes laborious years and hard work. A willingness to be looked down upon by other people. To be called crazy or insane. Why do we do this? Because the average life isn't for you. You want more than your situation. Whatever that may be, be patient, everything will come together.

278. **We're trapped inside ourselves. Only you can be the one to break free** ~ What you do and think, so shall your life become. If you think poorly of yourself, then you're going to have a bad life. Understand that where you grew up or where you come from doesn't define who you have to be. 80% of the millionaires out there today are self-made. We each have limitations put on ourselves. But guess what, you can overcome them. Stop lying to yourself. The way to get rid of negative thoughts is to take massive action. I don't care if today's Sunday, you're still going to work your ass off.

279. **We cannot become who we want by remaining who we are** ~ That voice telling you can't do it will be with you every step of your journey. Either you can listen to it or you can break free from it. It's not easy and you're going to have to work at it. We make up these excuses in our mind for why we can't achieve the task at hand. One way to break through your paradigms is to create a plan. Something that I call a fear list. Tape it where you can see it every day. Start with 10 things that scare the sh*t out of you. Create a plan to accomplish each one and your life will start to change before your eyes.

280. **Some people are old at 18 and some are young at 90. Age is a concept that humans created** ~ Saying old people are mature and young people are ignorant is false. Old means nothing other than what you look like on the outside and how long you've been alive. The only thing that truly matters is who you are on the inside and how you live your life. You could easily be in your 20s and have more wisdom and accomplishments than someone in their 90s. Why? Because you live your life in a better way and you respect your time. Alexander the Great took over the known world by 32, accomplishing what no other man, no matter how old had ever done. The point is never to say, 'I'm too young/too old." Age is bullsh*t. Your mindset is the only thing that matters in this world, so protect it at all costs.

281. **Beautiful faces are everywhere, but beautiful minds are hard to find** ~ There is beauty around us at all times. But how often does that beauty hide the individual? You can be the best-looking person in the world, but have the worst personality. You can be negative and tell yourself how life's not fair. You critique others and become judgmental. What about that person who sees the light in everything; who has faith that everything that happens to us happens for a reason? Sometimes you won't be able to understand why, but over time you will. Trust yourself that everything is going to work out. Be the positive light for others. Complaining takes too much time, look for the good in every situation. It's there for you to find it.

282. **If you get tired, learn to rest, not to quit** ~ We all get exhausted. This doesn't mean that you have to quit. Take a day off here and there to refresh your mind and come back even better. Promise yourself a treat at the end of the day when you're done grinding. This will make the grind that much easier. Whether it's going for a walk, making your favorite meal, or reading a novel you enjoy. When you have something to look forward to, you're going to push yourself that much more. If you feel burned out, take a 2-hour break. When you come back, you'll feel ready to conquer the world. Listen to your body and what it's telling you. I will never tell you to stop completely, only to re-charge and come back stronger.

283. **Don't think about the million reasons why it won't work. Think about the one reason it will** ~ To become the top in anything or to become the strongest version of yourself will require total self-belief. Throughout your journey, there will be obstacles, problems, and major setbacks, but it is not the setbacks themselves that gives them power, it is what you do about it that gives them power. You need to believe deep down that you will succeed, you can have no doubts. Why? Because it is so hard, which is why you should surround yourself with winners and not losers who complain and b*tch at every chance. You are going after your vision and you will make it a reality through you, so get serious and get to work.

284. **In business, not making a move is considered a move** ~ Once you have a business, everything you do is considered a move to the outside world. You need to know this. This also goes for life in general. By choosing not to say anything when someone is saying something against you, you are actually saying something and making a move; you are saying you don't want to deal with it or that you are above the situation. It all depends on their perspective, which is a scary thought, but true. The moral is: Plan your life and your every move before you make it and learn to view the situation from their point of view.

285. **Friends: I never see you at the club. Me: I never see you at the bank** ~ How many friends do you have who are always hitting you up about going out every weekend? Chances are, a lot. And chances are you go out with them every now and then, if not every time they ask. Why? Because you are in the wrong social group. If you want to reach the top while becoming the strongest version of yourself, you have no right to go out and celebrate for merely surviving the week. No, you will need to say 'I am busy' to your friends and continue the grind and just know that your 'friends' won't understand. But they will understand in 10 years when you are the head of your self-made empire while they are just getting by in life and living for temporary pleasure. Sacrifice now and live a life of freedom later.

286. **Once you feel you are avoided by someone, never disturb them again** ~ People will always be coming and going in your life. Only a small number that should stick around for long. People may call you cold-hearted. If I see no use for you in my life, why would I still want to talk to you? I only surround myself with the top individuals, people who don't b*tch and complain when times are tough. I have people who are going to push me to greater heights. Someone who's as hungry as I am. I don't care for games, if you leave, you leave. Understand that not everyone has a place in your life. You might hold onto someone for a while, then feel the need to kick them out. That's totally okay. This is your life; look out for your best interests.

287. **If you don't learn how to make money in your sleep, you will work until you die** ~ Do you really think that you're going to get the life that you want working for someone else? This is the middle-class mindset. If you want to be wealthy, you must be willing to work for yourself. You can try to climb up the corporate ladder for 10 years or you can grind day in and day out for 10 years. Push your worries to the side. Throw yourself out there, failure doesn't matter. When you're in your 20s is when you need to grind the most. Instead of partying every single weekend, how about staying in and working on your personal development? Life is about constant growth. If you aren't growing, you're dying.

288. **Never let someone waste your time twice** ~ Your time is valuable. And chances are that it's a lot more valuable than most people's time. Why? Because you have goals. You have a vision. And you have actually laid out your life in such a way that you will achieve greatness; but the truth is that the masses have no idea what you are even talking about or why you live your life like you do. They lack vision, goals, and any sense of the concept that time is limited. Knowing this, you must be ruthless with your time. Don't surround yourself with people who love wasting their own time because they will never value your time. And your time is more important than anything, so stay away from life's losers.

289. **Money won't make you happy, but neither will being broke** ~ People will tell you that money is bad. The people that tell you that don't have any. Let me tell you first-hand, being wealthy is a lot better than being poor. I can travel anywhere I want, I don't have to stress and budget like everyday people. I use that money to make more money. It's a simple process and one that has allowed me to live life on my own terms. People will say that money is bad for no reason at all. I provide jobs. I contribute to charities. What's wrong is that you're a consumer, not a producer. You're another cog in the machine, but it doesn't have to be that way. It's your life, so make the decisions that are going to allow you to become rich.

290. **It's not about the cards you're dealt, but how you play the hand** ~ Live by this rule: Control what you can control and forget about what you can't control. Problems, situations, and circumstances will come up in your life that you can't control, but what you can control, is how you will deal with them, you can either choose to complain and whine like a sheep or get sh*t done like a Lion. It's a choice, and it's one that we need to make daily. Are you going to b*tch or are you going to be proactive and not let things outside your control affect you? Control what you can and don't let other people or the situation control you. Be a Lion and do the best with what you are facing.

291. **We weren't put here to play games, we were put here to dominate** ~ Find me a person who doesn't want to dominate every aspect of their life; wealth, relationships, fitness, and spiritual. Most people are just playing the game, taking life as it comes to them. Lions would never wait for an opportunity to come to them. They're busting their asses trying to dominate not only the competition, but themselves as well. They're always looking to get stronger. When most people are complaining about their situation, you're working on creating your legacy. You weren't put here to play by society's rules; create your own and dominate along the way.

292. **Five By Five Rule: If it's not going to matter in five years, don't spend more than five minutes being upset by it** ~ Stop worrying about things that mean nothing or things that may never happen. So many of us get caught up in worrying about nothing. We think about what if this doesn't happen, what if that happens, what if I make this decision, etc., but the fact is that 90% of what you worry about every day will never even happen. It's just a waste of time. So start focusing on what you can control and stop thinking about what is out of your control. There is only so much time in the day and you need to use every minute of it wisely.

293. **The comeback is always greater than the setback** ~ After a setback, are you willing to get back up? When you get punched in the face over and over again, you're going to get beaten to your knees, but guess what: You have to be the one to pull yourself up. You can't expect other people to provide for your family. You can't expect other people to make your dreams come true. That is all on you and it will always be on you! You have the choice every single day to work towards your dreams or take another step back. I understand it isn't easy, but you have to break through it.

294. **If they don't know you personally, don't take it personally** ~ How many of you get offended by what so-and-so says about you? Or what someone on social media says about you? Well, you shouldn't; you should only care about what your true friends and close family think of you, and even that should be limited. So stop wasting valuable time keeping up to date with what this or that person is saying about you. You have more important things to do. Let them think whatever the hell they want; it doesn't change who you are or what you stand for. You need to realize that life's losers have nothing better to do than point out faults in others, so let them. They are sheep and Lions do not care about their opinion.

295. A man who masters patience masters everything else ~ Welcome to the 21st century, aka the century of instant gratification. People today want things now but do not want to work for them. People want to live the luxury life, yet are not willing to grind to get there. Why? Because we have lost our focus and patience. With today's distractions, we cannot be patient and trust the process. We get sidetracked and want results now; this is a sheep mentality, so if you have it, lose it. You are entitled to nothing in this life, and if you want something, you need to put in the hours to get it and never lose your patience because it's 'taking too long.' It's only taking too long because you slack off and are inconsistent and jump into every new project and never stay with one for long. It's time to get serious.

296. Family is the most important thing you can have in life ~ Family is an essential asset in building your dreams. They may not see the world the way you do, but that's certainly okay. They'll always be there for you, but you need to make time for them. As entrepreneurs, we're constantly busy with a never-ending to-do list. With all the hustle, sometimes we need to slow down and appreciate those around us. Take one night or a few hours per week and spend time with your loved ones. This is your life and it's ending one minute at a time. Strive for constant important in all areas of your life.

297. Set a goal. Write it down. Take daily action. Smash your goal ~ Why is writing your goal on paper so easy to do, yet so hard to actually accomplish? It's because you are a sheep. Sheep rarely write their goals down, and the few sheep that do usually just forget about it in a week. But that isn't you. You are the rare Lion among sheep, and when a Lion writes a goal down, they will work like hell to accomplish it. They won't fool around or let their particular 'circumstance' dictate if they are going to get their goal done. Why? Because when they write a goal, they go after it with everything they have.

298. **Never forget who was there for you when no one else was** ~ There is no shortage of people who want to be around you when you are successful, but there is a shortage of people when you are broke with nothing but a dream. Many of the most successful people in the world are still close to those who were with them at the bottom. Why? Because they know those people like them for them and not the superficial status they may have now. Keep them in your life and never forget how much they helped and comforted you during the hard times of the grind. They are irreplaceable. And one more piece of advice: once you reach the top, beware of a lot of fake people.

299. **It takes nothing to join the crowd. It takes everything to stand alone** ~ The common notoriety in today's society is to follow the pack. You're looked down upon if you want to better yourself. It's typical to hate your job, it's typical to complain about your life because 99% of the population does it. Do you not understand that this is your life? Instead of b*tching and moaning about your circumstance, why don't you try and fix it? You get paid what you're worth. If you come home and watch TV, well, your worth isn't going to be that high. If you're constantly improving, reading, learning, your income is going to increase as time goes on. Stand alone, even if it means leaving everyone else behind.

300. **Dress for the job you want, not the job you have** ~ I'm going to be blunt. People judge you by your appearance. If you're wearing sweatpants and a sweatshirt, what are people going to think of you? What about if you're wearing a suit, and clean-shaven? Everyone is going to take you more seriously. You don't have to be lavish and buy top-dollar suits, just something that makes you look respectable. You're personifying your brand every time you step outside the door. What are you saying to the world? When you dress for the life you want, your subconscious mind is going to activate.

301. **The broke stay broke because they pretend to be rich** ~ Have you been trying to become wealthy for a long time but still haven't? Then you need to take a hard and objective look at what you do day to day, how much you spend per day and what your priorities are. And if you are not making a lot of money, why are you always going out and buying the best of clothes, furniture and takeout? It doesn't make sense. If you are doing this, your values are not aligned with your lifestyle. You need to be frugal. You need to say 'F*ck the luxury lifestyle,' any spare money is going to go towards buying assets, not liabilities.

302. **Anyone can start a business, but few will succeed** ~ Are you going to be one of those people who succeed? It's no secret that people don't like starting a business. The population would rather work for someone else once the business has been established. If you want to get out of the rat race, be willing to work 80 hours per week. People say that they want to start a business for more free time. This couldn't be further from the truth. You have to become obsessed with what you're doing. You're going to be spending every waking minute thinking about or working on your business. It becomes an addiction, but only if you succeed.

303. **I hate math but love counting money** ~ I don't care for useless knowledge. As a matter of fact, if you're not teaching me how to better myself or make money, I don't care what you say. In schools, they teach you about functions and pointless bullsh*t. What about asset allocation? How about learning from Ray Dalio? They don't care for that. Because we employ people with the middle-class mindset. We send kids off to school to spend $1,000 on a class when they could spend $0.25 on overdue fees at the library. The patriarchal society we live in is coming to an end. The difference between the middle and upper class is growing every day. You have to take it upon yourself to build wealth.

304. **You save your money to party on the weekends. I save it to build my empire. We are never going to be the same** ~ We all have to make choices in our life. Are you thinking about how you're spending your money for the weekend or spending your money to grow? This is your life. You are the one who dictates how your money will be spent. Too many of us care about instant gratification and looking towards the weekend, instead of looking towards the future. When are you going to start taking responsibility for everything in your life? Quit putting the blame on others. Don't care about what others are doing with their money. You have to be the one to care about you and you only.

305. **My goal is not to be better than anyone else, but better than I used to be** ~ I focus on myself. You can't force people to change themselves; they have to be willing to do it on their own. The person you can change is yourself. We're constantly changing every day for better and for worse. Are you reading every day? Most people come home from work and relax instead of working on themselves. I understand it's hard, but how are you going to get a better life if you don't improve? You have to work harder on yourself than you do on your job. Strive to be a better person. In order to achieve more, you have to become more.

306. **You're never too important to be nice to people** ~ It's hard to be successful. But it's a whole other ballgame if you are trying to reach the top in your industry. Why? Because it's a level reserved for only the elite: Life's legends and life's Lions. And if you want to reach that echelon of success, you need to be and stay humble. You need to be grounded. You need to let go of your ego and feeling of self-importance, because that is the number one killer of successful people. Successful people of success start failing when they think they are all that and better than everyone else. Never have this mindset. Always be working on your character and develop a moral code, then abide by it.

307. **Happiness comes from positive moments and loving people** ~ Happiness is a choice. Only you can look at the world in light or darkness. Are you going to see that everything that happens to you happens for a reason? Or are you going to complain about a situation that you can't fix. When something goes wrong in your life, don't get upset: Figure out a remedy for the problem. A loser complains. A winner fixes the situation. It's not easy at times, but if you connect the dots looking backwards, it will almost always make sense. While going through life, throw off a positive vibe to everyone you know. Be people-friendly and love deeply.

308. **The world is a jungle. You either fight or run forever** ~ It's hard to pave your own path in life. Why? Almost no one does it. They are not willing to fight for their individuality. They want to be like everyone else and accept mediocrity and the average as their life's outcome. They are robots and will detest change. Know this: The masses are sheep and not Lions. You can either choose to give into society's sheep standards or you can choose to say f*ck it, I'm creating my own life by developing an ultimate vision and working towards it every day.

309. **In the end, we all discover who's fake, who's true and who would risk it all for you** ~ When you start your journey, there will be people who stay with you and people who leave. When you get to the top, there will be people who like you for your fame and fortune, nothing more than that. Looking back, you know who was with you the entire time. They started on your journey and they came with you. Keep the real people close. They'll be hard to find once you're at the top. Life's not easy and you shouldn't be worrying about who to trust or not. Some guys and girls will like you for your money. Keep silent when you first meet and many nights thereafter. Attract others with your personality and they'll stick around.

310. It kills people when they don't know your business. Stay private ~ If you are trying to become a huge sensation in the public's eye, this advice isn't necessary. But for all of you quiet Lions building your own empires, this is mandatory. You should always be quiet, reserved, and private about your goals, the moves you're making, and what you do day-to-day to build your empire. The world has no right to know, but they will absolutely want to know after you reached a certain level of success, and you staying quiet will make you that much more interesting. Keep to yourself and stay true to your ultimate vision. This is your life and you need to make it happen. Be committed to the grind and not the publicity.

311. Never be controlled by three things: Your past, money, or people ~ Don't let anyone or anything define who you are. Your past, money situation, or people in your life don't define you. You define you. We all started at the bottom and we worked our way up. It wasn't handed to us, we busted our ass for it. While you were sleeping, we were grinding. While you were partying, we were learning. Your past doesn't have to define your future. You can make a choice to say that enough is enough and that you're going to change. There's going to be a point in your life when you're sick and tired of where you are and you long for more out of life. Don't let what happened in the past cloud your mind for the future.

312. Money fills your pocket. Adventure fills your soul ~ Money is important. It may be the most important thing besides family and relationships; but why? Because money allows you to travel, to spend unlimited time with loved ones, and to do anything else you want. That is why you must be obsessed with money and use it as your slave so that you can make money while you sleep. Adventure, vacations, and time with friends and family are what life's about, and the best life is about unlimited freedom to adventure throughout the world. So, if you want to live to your fullest potential, take money every week from your paycheck (if you work) and invest it in assets that will produce income while you sleep.

313. **If you want to reach the top you need to have grit** ~ Want to reach the top in your industry while becoming the strongest version of yourself? Then you must have grit. Grit is something that every legendary person has. Grit is the inner power that makes you work towards your ultimate vision while giving zero excuses or taking breaks because you don't feel like working today. Grit is the most powerful trait because it makes a person unstoppable. So, if you want to reach the top, develop a vision and work on it while never b*tching or complaining like the sheep of the world.

314. **Whenever you feel like giving up, think about all the people who would love to see you fail** ~ There will be times when you will doubt yourself. It happens to the best of us, but guess what: If you can change your thinking, you can change your life. No matter what obstacles you face in this world, they can be overcome. I don't care who you are or where you're from. There is someone out there who was in a much tougher situation than you're in who has become successful. They didn't b*tch or moan about their life, they found a way. They continuously worked each and every day, including the weekends. Remember all the people who said you couldn't do it. All the people who laughed at you and told you that you'd never achieve your dreams? Who's the one laughing now?

315. **Everyone wants to be a beast until it's time to do what beasts do** ~ You can talk as much as you want, but are you going to back it up? Are you going to show results instead of excuses? We all have hopes and dreams in this world, but you have to be willing to do the work. I don't care who you are or where you come from, if you want to be successful, you're going to have to grind. Yes, it might be hard at times. But do you know what's also hard? Being broke. Quit always talking about what you're going to do and start actually doing it. Grind in silence and let your results speak for you. Are you willing to sacrifice a few years to get the life you want?

316. **Most people don't change, they just find a new way to lie** ~ The wise do not blindly listen to people's words. They don't even fully believe the person's actions. They believe the person's pattern. Most people are set in their ways from years of the same habits and inclinations, so words and promises from a person mean relatively nothing and their actions could show you they mean it temporarily, but how long will it last? That's where patterns come in. Look at their past accomplishments and relationships and see what they look like. There will most likely be a pattern and that should be your only instrument to tell if that person is a liar or a person of character.

317. **Going after your dreams is like being on an island all by yourself** ~ When you're going after your dreams, welcome to the 1%. 99% of the population will hate what they're doing every day, but they won't do anything to change their situation. They think this is a normal way to live, but that isn't you, you know better! I understand that entrepreneurship can be lonely at times, that no one gets you. Well, you will never get them either. You understand the value of what it means to grind and pursue greatness. The sacrifices you are making today are going to grow in the future. Continue day in and day out. Once you get to be successful, it doesn't get any easier. Get used to it.

318. **Sometimes the King needs to show the sheep why he's King** ~As you grow in power and become a more successful person, your old friends will still think you are that same old person you've always been. They will delude themselves into thinking they deserve the great lifestyle and money that you now have and they will never truly understand why you have more than them. And do you know why you'll have more than them? It is because you worked. Instead of staying in the same place all your life, you have been working towards your ultimate vision. Never stagnant and never moving backwards. You don't ask for handouts or feel entitled because you value yourself and your work ethic. So make sure you are ready to show them you are not equals if the time comes for it. Because the time will come; and, when it comes, be prepared to act like a Lion to the many disillusioned sheep.

319. **The thing about smart people is that they sound crazy to dumb people** ~ When you're on another level in your life and you want to talk to the average mind, you won't be able to. You'll figure out a way to get out of the conversation. I don't have time to deal with petty talk, I'm focusing on making my dreams become a reality. You're going to be laughed at. You'll tell people that you're going to be a millionaire and they don't think it's possible; that's their limiting belief, not yours! If you want it bad enough, you'll work for it. If you believe it can be done, it can, and don't let anyone tell you otherwise. You're not going to be understood no matter what you do.

320. **Let them party. One day they will be working for you. ~** Always remember when you feel like you are 'done' and you want to go party, fool around and sleep in, that someone else is out there grinding and getting ahead. You are not against yourself until you are at the top. You are against everyone else in your industry. Sacrifice your years now and do not live for temporary pleasure like everyone else. Work hard and long every damn day and you will have a life of freedom and employ those that decided to party multiple times a week.

321. **A wounded Lion is still fiercer than a healthy sheep** ~ One of the main reasons why you are not successful yet is because you value comfort and safety over expansion! The majority of people love to do the same thing every day. They like their comfort zones and hate expanding into new territory or starting a new venture, which is why they are the majority. So if you want to be a part of life's legends, you are going to need to do the opposite. And that is trying new things, embracing change and the pain of evolving. It's a Lion habit. Lions know how to adapt and are not going to be and or stay in one place for the rest of their life.

322. **Every great warrior has to undergo serious opposition before they became a legend** ~ If you ever had thoughts of becoming a legend, you are on the right path. Why? Because a legend isn't made by chance. A legend is made by choice. A legend is not an average person—they hate average and also being above average; they seek to dominate their field. That is what being a legend is all about. So if you want to become one, plan to multiply your work ethic by 10 right now and wake up each morning ready to move forward in your life's odyssey.

323. **Be addicted to your passions, not your distractions** ~ An overwhelming number of people are addicted to their distractions. They're constantly on social media, not realizing exactly how much time they're spending. We're all addicted to something. For some it's good, but for most it's bad. What if you started to implement good habits? Start small, go one by one. Over time, these good habits will be implemented. Start to become addicted to your passions. We all have one deep down inside. To change the world, you first must change yourself.

324. **Don't be afraid of being outnumbered. Eagles fly alone. Pigeons fly together** ~The journey to the top in any industry is hard as hell. There is no way you will reach the top, or even come close, by following what everyone has always done and by obeying every single rule. Be prepared to break the rules and walk alone for most of it. On this journey, you will be up against the crowd, the sheep, the pigeons, the common people. They will harass you, call you names and say you are crazy. But you weren't born to be another sheep who follows orders and comes and leaves at a certain time each and every day. You are a Lion, an Eagle, a different type of person that doesn't give a sh*t about what 'they' do or what 'they' say. You are doing this for yourself, your family and your empire. Walk alone and do not follow the crowd of pigeons.

325. **A friendship founded on business is better than a business founded on friendship** ~ Do you know how many businesses started by friendship fail and their friendship is then lost? Too many. Why? They are too comfortable with each other and are so blinded by friendship that they cannot say what they want to say or do what they want to do. Never go into business with your close friends. It's just too hard to do and it's a fact that you will overlook some qualities because you are so close and comfortable with each other. Instead, go into business with someone who is qualified and self-motivated, someone who will be a great partner and one that you can be straight up with. You can call them out for not doing their part and you expect them to do the same. No love lost when you are not close friends.

326. **Strong women intimidate boys and excite men** ~ If you're a woman out there who's grinding, don't settle for just anyone. If you think that you're going to find a hardworking guy in the club, you're going to be too wrong. You have to find the person who complements what you're trying to achieve. We live in a world where 99% of people don't chase after their dreams. You're not one of those people and to expect to find the right person to date right away is unrealistic. Understand that being alone is far better than being with someone who brings you down. Go out there and meet and befriend as many people as you can. I guarantee you'll meet someone who's chasing his dream.

327. **I used to be afraid of being alone. Now I'm afraid of having the wrong people as company** ~At the beginning of your journey, you'll be afraid of being alone. This is the first time in your life where you're going against what society has told you to do. I remember I used to question myself, as if I was doing something wrong. Now, it couldn't be further from that. I look at others like something is wrong with them. They're content with average. Content on settling for less than they are capable of. I've learned it's better to walk alone than try to fit in with everyone else. There are other people out there who are as obsessed about self-improvement and success; you just have to look for them.

328. **I was raised to treat the janitor with the same respect as the CEO** ~ Nothing is more important than treating others with respect, especially those lower than you on the ladder of success. In life, it's easy to get caught up in your position and high success; you will be clouded by luxury and your ego will become bigger. This is all ok, but never let that affect the way you treat others. Everyone is fighting something in their life and they do not need you to make them feel worse than they might already feel. Besides that, disrespecting others just puts up a barrier to your network, so there is no benefit to it. So do not do it; be known as a class act.

329. **Winners always find a way to win** ~ Losing once is not being a loser. Losing 1000 times is not being a loser if they are grinding every day. A loser is someone who doesn't try, gives up, or lives a life filled with losing on every front. Lions are not losers. Lions find a way to win from any situation, either by learning from their losses or actually winning. It's all a learning experience and a way to get better. Lions take every negative and make it a positive. You must have this mindset and one day you will win most of your battles. Stay persistent towards working on your vision and one day it'll be yours.

330. **I usually give people more chances than they deserve, but once I'm done, I'm done** ~ So many of us, whether in a relationship with a boyfriend or girlfriend or just a friend relationship, believe that we can change the other person. We think that if we explain our way, they will understand. I guarantee you that it happens almost 0% of the time. You give someone chances over and over again. They say they're going to change. They change for a week, then they go back to their old habits. Is this someone that you really want in your life? You might cherish and love this person, but they need to be excluded from your life. You can only give someone so many chances.

331. **True leaders don't create followers, they create more leaders** ~ As a leader, you're going to have to tell the other person like it is. That person might not like what you're going to say, they may even hate you for it, but in the end they will be appreciative. I'd rather be hurt with the truth than comforted with a lie. True leaders don't tell people what they need to do, they show them in person. They do whatever it takes to help that person. Creating followers does nothing. You have to influence that person to take action. Without action, nothing will be accomplished. A leader creates other leaders. Someone who can spread his wisdom and make it to known to the entire world.

332. **In this world there is no shortage of money, just a shortage of people who think big enough** ~ If you are not financially successful, you are not thinking big enough. Becoming financially successful is one of the hardest things to do, especially if you didn't come from money. Why? You have innate barriers formed in your mind, so you might think it's too difficult for your circumstances, but you would be wrong. It's time to think 10 times bigger. You need to read the major success stories of the many immigrants and poor people who become modern-day-titans by nothing but sheer big thinking and a relentless work ethic. The time is now for you to become the next titan. Get to work.

333. **What you have done is nothing compared to what you can do** ~ The only way to truly be successful is to never be satisfied with your current accomplishments and where you are in life. The minute you get complacent is the start of your end. As you grow and progress as a person, your big goals will now seem small to you. The only way that you can keep going is stay hungry. Set goals that are outrageous to you right now. You're going to have to grow into that person to obtain those goals. It isn't going to be easy. But what's the point of living if you are already dead on the inside? Why not make as big an impact as you can?

334. **Be so busy improving yourself that you have no time to criticize others** ~Focus on yourself and where you want to go in life. You're not here to impress anyone or cater to anyone's needs. People buy items they can't afford to impress people they don't like. Do what makes you happy. Seek approval from yourself and no one else. You have to love yourself first before someone else can fall in love with you. We can go our entire lives doing things just to impress or seek approval. This is the greatest mistake that you can make. Get comfortable being an outlier. You're not like the rest of the 99%. You're the 1% for a reason, so act like it.

335. **Before you give up, think how far you will be next year if you don't** ~ A little progress is still more progress than the person who has done nothing. Sometimes we get caught up with others' successes that we forget to see how far we've come. What you are doing is amazing. If you're chasing your dreams and not letting anyone tell you what you can and can't, you're on the right path. You will have up and downs, but it's all going to be worth it. If you achieve your dreams in three years from now, are you going to really care that it took that long? No, you're going to be thankful for what you have. You know the sacrifices and dedication that you put in to accomplish what you set out to do. Never stop improving and never stop setting the bar higher.

336. **Exams and grades are temporary, but education is permanent** ~ If you are being educated only in school, then you are not educated at all. You can read about starting a business, but until you actually start, nothing is going to get done. No idea is perfect; you just need to start. You're going to learn more in one year of self-education and business than you would in 16 years of formal schooling. There are tons of successful people who never went to college, or who never even finished high school. You have no excuse. There is someone out there living the life you want to live. Success leaves clues; just do as they say and never be satisfied. Be constantly learning, listening, and watching what others are doing. To become successful, it starts with what you're reading and watching every day.

337. **I am mature enough to forgive you, but not dumb enough to trust you again** ~ I've always been one to forgive, but never to forget. I don't care who you are, if you wronged me, I will remember. I don't hate you because that takes too much energy. I remember what you said and that gives me a little more motivation when I need it. You may think that I forgot, but I didn't. I'm never going to allow you back into my life with open arms. The people who are dumb enough to let you back in amaze me. They're like the people who fail, but continue the same strategy over and over—it's never going to work.

338. **Being happy is an inside job, remember that** ~ How can someone be mad all the time? We all know that one person who's always pissed, complaining and blaming everyone for their life but their self. They never take responsibility. They are always unhappy. Well, newsflash: You control and are responsible for your life and your emotions. It's a choice to be happy and it's a choice to be productive... Stop blaming everything and everybody but yourself and accept where you are, and if you don't like it, work to change your position. There are many people who are impoverished, who didn't come from privilege, who come from broken homes and they still choose to be happy.

339. **Everybody you fight is not your enemy, and everybody that you help is not your friend** ~ In business and in life, you always need to be aware. Aware of people who try to manipulate, take control, and put you down. You need to understand that, as you grow in success, you will be hunted more, not less, and that means that every person you help is not your friend, you are just a good person. But never trust them. And that goes for people you fight, whether they are on your side or the person on the other side of the deal: They are not your enemy. Stay neutral. Keep your close friends close and know who your enemies are or potential enemies are at all times. For the social scene is not a black-and-white game, there is a grey area.

340. **Some people aren't your friends, they're just scared to be your enemy** ~ As you grow in success and in power, this will be your reality. Be prepared for the fakes, the snakes who wear an exterior of friendliness just to get things from you. Know that they will be there and learn how to spot them. If you let them get close to you, they will take everything you've accomplished and use it for themselves. Always make sure you know who's your ally and your enemy.

341. **If your goals set you apart from the crowd, stay alone** ~ Are you taking today off or are you grinding? The majority of people never set goals in their lives; they let whatever happens to them just happen. They think that others should decide how to live life for them. Where you want to be is made up of the choices you make. No one is holding you back from yourself. If you're hanging out with people whose goals aren't as enticing as yours are, it's time to find new people. Don't give me the excuse that it's hard. What's hard is living a life less than you deserve. It's never going to be easy so stop complaining and start working.

342. **Being a real gentleman never goes out of style** ~ Being a man of class never goes out of style. All this modern 'swag' nonsense, treating people badly, and being a punk is not cool. What is cool is being a gentlemen, a Lion, at a time where being one is becoming a lost art. It doesn't matter how poor or rich you are. It doesn't matter how powerful you are or what your position is in life. You can still act like a real man. A gentleman is a man who has mastery over his emotions, treats others with respect, and is a leader. They don't put people down. They don't complain like sheep. They are Lions. Join us in the movement to bring chivalry and the art of the gentleman back into society by starting with yourself.

343. **While others are sleeping, partying, and fooling around, I am grinding** ~ If you are not yet successful, why would you waste time? It's a simple question. The answer is: You shouldn't. What you should be doing is grinding every day until you are successful. Put in the work regardless of how you feel. Also, you should never feel like you are missing out because you are not. You are working for something greater. You are sacrificing pleasure now for greatness and freedom in your later life. Leave it to the sheep of the world to party, fool around, and sleep in. You've got your goals to go after.

344. **You can never be overdressed or overeducated** ~ There are some things in life that you can have too much of. Being overdressed or overeducated isn't one of them. How you dress and what you wear tells the world a lot about you. It's also no secret that the average CEO reads 60 books per year compared to less than one book per year for the average employee. People will tell you that you overdress and they will tell you to stop reading. It's because you intimidate them. They want to be you or at least bring you down to their level. When you go through life, never stop learning and never stop dressing as nice as you want. Life is simple, don't over-complicate it.

345. You're not rich until you have something that money can't buy ~ Money can buy all sorts of things, but it can't buy you happiness. It can get you close, but lead you down a never-ending trail of more. Money can't buy you a family and kids. True happiness is when you love what you do without getting paid. What would you do right now if you had all the money in the world? Just because you have tons of money doesn't guarantee your happiness. Yes, it can buy you a boat, a golf membership, whatever you picture in your wildest dreams. Money becomes a fixture for people. They think that once they get it, they'll be happy. Why not be happy for what you have? Why not show gratitude for every gift that has been given to you in your life?

346. I don't need you to believe in me, I believe in me ~ If you don't believe in yourself, how is everyone else supposed to believe in you? You think that becoming dependent on another person is going to satisfy you, how illogical is that? You have to put yourself first. Why wait to take that trip with another person? Just go by yourself. It might be scary, but at least you'll grow from it. You have to have a relationship with yourself. You have to invest in yourself 100% and not let anything or anyone dictate how you're going to live. Praise yourself when you accomplish a goal. Treat and connect with yourself, you'll start to gain confidence. Once you gain the confidence, anything is possible.

347. Your life is like a movie. You write the script. Will it be a hit or a flop? It's all up to you ~ Your life is your life. You may not control your start, but you sure as hell control your middle and your ultimate outcome. Stop blaming everyone else for where you are and complaining about your current or past situation. Doing that produces nothing but negativity. The real question you need to ask yourself is: What do you want to be remembered for? What is the outcome of your movie, your life? It's time to write your life's script. Get serious. You and only you are in control of your life—make it a legendary one.

348. Inside every person is a beast that is waiting to be unleashed ~ Whatever level you are at, you can do better. It doesn't matter if you are working all day every day, you could be doing better. You could be using your time more wisely and working smarter. It's time to unleash your inner beast, the Lion that sits inside you just waiting to come out. it's that quiet voice inside your head that says you can work a little harder and a little longer than your mind is telling you. Show the world what you can do.

349. **The more you know about life, business, and power the dumber you sound to stupid people** ~ For the most part, this is true of our generation. Our generation is the social media generation, the temporary pleasure generation. Most people believe almost anything they read as a meme or on any news outlet because they would rather be led by someone than form their own opinion. They would rather fill their minds with stupid information and updates on celebrity gossip. This is the world for most people, but the good news is that, if you are a Lion, you can use this to your advantage. How? By focusing on things that actually matter, such as accomplishing goals, reading, and learning. In essence, do not be deterred by the sheep of the world, for they are going nowhere if they do not implement the habits of Lions.

350. **A year from now, we'll see who was really working** ~ People will talk time and time again about what they're going to do. That's fine, but show me results. Are you taking action every day? Are you working on the weekends? Are you getting up early and grinding? Tons of people say they're going to be successful, but do you have what it takes? When something doesn't go right or a failure arises, how are you going to respond? We all have choices. We all have the same 24 hours in a day. Why is it that some people are successful and some people aren't? How you use your time today will dictate the life you're living a year from now.

351. **The differences between men and boys are the lessons they learn** ~ You can take what you learn and you can apply it in your life or you can let it pass. Are you learning from others? Seeing how they see things? Or are you learning from those who are below you? Do you know what drink, what not to drink, and what asset not to buy? It's simple. There are people who are 60, but still children. Are you providing for and protecting your family? There are more boys out in the world than there are men. Men take responsibility for their life. They don't care what others think of them. They make their own moves and do what's best for them. Are you going to be a man among boys? The choice is up to you.

352. **Sacrifice a few years of partying for a decade of freedom** ~ If you want to be massively successful when you are older, you need to be willing to put in the work now. In your younger years, it's easy to goof off, party and take weekends and nights off. Almost everyone does it and it's the cool thing to do. It's weird to be different. It's weird to want more and to have huge ambitions. But, guess what, everyone who f*cked around in their 20s and 30s is paying the price now while the people who ground every damn day in their younger years have an empire and complete freedom. So the question is: Are you willing to sacrifice temporary pleasure for freedom and greatness? That answer will determine your destiny.

353. **Confuse them with your silence and amaze them with your actions** ~ We all know this type of person: All talk and no results. These people are rampant throughout society. They love to talk about their future plans, but fail to act on those plans to make them more than just plans, and some of them just blame others for their lack of success. Well, I'm here to tell you that Lions do not do this. Lions let their results speak for themselves. Lions speak little but are well-known for their results because they are life's action-takers. They don't give a sh*t about people's opinions of them because they actually produce results and can accomplish their goals. It's time to stay quiet and it's time to take massive action.

354. **Quiet people have the loudest minds** ~ The people who talk the least are the ones you should be most afraid of. They keep to their ideas, planning to perfect them each second. You mistake their quietness as a weakness. In turn, you're the weak one. When you speak your mind, they remember every intricate detail. They get the ways you do business out of you. They don't speak unless they're spoken to. Silences don't affect those who don't care about what others think of them. You're going to cast these people aside. They'll be quietly working day in and day out. You won't see it. It'll take time, you'll get comfortable, and then they'll dethrone you.

355. **If you can count your money, you don't have enough** ~ Do you ever notice that the people who can count their money complain the most? They have to worry about bills and can take only one vacation per year. You see, you should be having so many income streams that you forget where it's all coming from. If you know the exact amount of money in your bank account right now, you need more. Why not try to make as much as you can? You're not doing a service to anyone by being broke. Who are you helping out? No one, and that's selfish. Having massive amounts of money means that you'll be able to help those in need. You can look after more than yourself. You can provide jobs for other people. It's selfish not making as much as you can.

356. **Keep your moves silent, your money invested, and your life low-key** ~ Keep people on their toes, always guessing what you're going to do next. Every day that you keep moving forward, they stay complacent. When you're looking for new investment opportunities to put your money to work, they're leaving it in a bank. They announce what they're doing or what they plan to do. They're playing chess while you're playing checkers. A true Lion lies low. You may not notice what they've accomplished, but it adds up over time. You think they're the same person, but that's only you. Move with silence and leave them in awe.

357. **Risking is always better than regretting** ~ Do you want to live your entire life without taking any chances? When you're on your deathbed, you don't want to have regrets. To live a fulfilling and exciting life, you have to do what scares you. That could be taking a trip to somewhere you've never been before or even going alone. It's not going to be easy, nor will it ever be. If it frightens you, do it. Take the chance and never look back. Keep your eye on the present and what you have to look forward to. I recommend doing one thing every day that scares you. It could be progressing into unknown territory or making an extra sales call. If you're constantly taking risks and improving yourself, you'll never look back with regret.

358. **If you keep putting things off until tomorrow, before you know it years have gone by** ~ How many of you have written down your goals and then forgot about them a few weeks later? Chances are almost every one of you. Why? Because goal setting has become soft. The concept of goal setting should be almost permanent. You should spend hours planning and making goals and then work like hell to accomplish them. You shouldn't be changing your goals every single day or worse, forgetting about them. That's a sheep move. Lions, on the other hand, write down their goals and then do whatever it takes in order to get them done.

359. **I don't care who the biggest fish in the pond is. I'm a whole different animal** ~ If you want to reach the top, you need to know your competition. You need to keep track of what moves they are making and have a close eye on those rising up. But the most important ingredient for you to be a part of the elite is: strongly and absolutely believing you are destined for greatness. You need to fully believe that you are going to be number one. It's not cocky. It's a necessary self-belief and you are going to need the work ethic to get there. So wake up tomorrow fully believing in your greatness.

360. **The sky isn't the limit, your vision is** ~A powerful quote from the book *Think and Grow Rich*: "Whatever the mind can conceive and believe, it can achieve." I want you to think of your ultimate vision. Now I want you to know that it is within your grasp. The problem with most people is that their minds are filled with limited beliefs, mediocre thoughts, and a small vision. It's the way most of us have grown up, taught by 'adults' who think they know what's best for us because they are 'older.' Well, the truth is, unless they are doing what you want to do with your life their advice is meaningless. You need to pave your own path. You need to adamantly believe that you can achieve your vision. You must be bold. It's time to think bigger and to multiply your vision by 10.

361. **Patience is power** ~ Patience is an art form that most people lack. We live in a fast-paced world where we expect things to be done right away. You start a business and think you're going to be a millionaire within six months. Unless you're an outlier, it will take years of dedication and grit to achieve that goal. Focus on today. What can do you do that's going to get you closer to your goal? Be improving yourself and your business. Over time, this will add up to your success.

362. **I used to walk into a room and wonder if they liked me. Now I wonder if I like them** ~ This is the power of becoming your own person. Someone you are proud of being because you know how much work you put into yourself over the years. You have respect for yourself and you realize who you are today is not an accident. Who you are today is based on everything you have done in your past—and if you don't like who you are, change!

363. **The only thing that I am committed to right now is bettering myself** ~ There is nothing selfish about working on yourself. You should be taking time every day to be alone to work on your inner self and your vision. You should be reading books, setting goals, and moving forward. This is your one life. You don't get a second chance, so why would you not consciously work on yourself day in and day out, becoming the best you could be? It's time to get started; or, if you have already gotten started, it's time to do more.

364. **Your mind is your strongest muscle and your worst enemy** ~ Your mind is your most dangerous weapon. It can be your most powerful ally or it can be your worst enemy. It controls how you see the world and what you do every day. If you ever want to reach the top and or become the strongest version of yourself, you will need to take full control over your mind. Do not make decisions while you're drunk, angry or horny. You must have a clear head. You must be reading powerful books and learning all that you can about your craft. You need to be writing your vision down every day so it is ingrained inside of you. And remember, "Program your mind or it will be programmed by life."

365. **Successful people blame nobody but themselves for their mistakes** ~ Are you willing to take full responsibility for your life? If you're in a job you hate, whose fault is that? If you're in a relationship you don't like, get out of it. No one is telling you what to do. Who's running your life, you or someone else? If you don't make choices for yourself, someone else will make them for you. Quit complaining and saying that the world isn't fair. We all have it hard. It's going to be even harder if you blame others. You are the direct cause of everything in your life. Once you can grasp that concept, you can start to live the life you wish.

366. **When life gets harder, challenge yourself to be stronger** ~ There are two things you can do when your life gets hard. You can give up, which will then make it easier for you to give up again and again or you can push through and go even harder. The choice is yours. And most people will quit and go back to watching television. But those select few, the Lions of the world, will face them head on. You welcome chaos, problems, and difficult situations because it is during those times when you grow in your character, skills, and overall mindset. It's time for you to step your game up and believe that you can overcome any obstacle.

367. **Loyalty isn't grey. It's black and white. You're either completely loyal or not loyal at all** ~ Loyalty takes years to create and a second to break. It is one of those rare qualities that very few people actually possess. Why? Because it's hard. It's hard to pledge your loyalty to someone or something and then, when something better comes along, it's hard to resist it. But a person of true character does resist. Once a person of character makes a promise, they stick with it. They don't let the circumstance or the person dictate how they will respond to their promise. And if that type of person is you, a person of character, you are dangerous to the outside world. Dangerous because they know that, once you say something, you mean it, which is a lost art in today's world.

368. **Don't be afraid to be alone. Don't be afraid to like it** ~ If you can be comfortable being alone, you have an advantage over everyone. Your happiness need not depend on someone else. Do what makes you happy and what gives you joy. Don't be afraid to escape from the herd and go off on your own. You must make sacrifices... And most of the time, you'll be walking alone.

369. **Don't be afraid about starting small. There are valuable lessons in humble beginnings** ~ If you weren't born into a rich and powerful family, good. Most of the children from these types of families feel entitled, possess a poor work ethic, and are cocky. They haven't developed the resilience that growing up in a humble beginning requires. Their life has been easy and they have, for the most part, been sheltered from the world. Use this to your advantage. You know what it feels like to be at a low level of success. You have ground from the bottom and are on a mission to reach the top. You will become a self-made person. So never feel self-pity. Be thankful for the way you grew up. "With every disadvantage, there is an opposite advantage."

370. **My time, my money, and my respect are not to be f*cked with** ~ We only have so much time on this planet, why would you ever let someone waste your time? Time is the only commodity you can never get back. Only invest in ideas and business opportunities that you see are going to make you money. If you're not smart about where you put it, you'll end up broke. You need to protect your family, no matter what it takes. That might mean going to battle or war with someone else. Lastly, don't ever let anyone disrespect you. If they do, stand your ground. Punch them in the face; it doesn't matter if you lose, at least you stood up for yourself.

371. **Before you ask why someone hates you, ask yourself why you give a f*ck** ~ Does so and so hate me? Does he/she really not like me? These are the types of questions that misguided people constantly ask. They are so focused on what other people think of them that they can never truly become their own person. We were all meant to shine as children, to be an individual, and to be unique. We were not meant to follow the crowd nor blindly conform to society's standards. And if someone hates you for living life on your own terms, let them. They have time to waste while you do not. Stay focused.

372. **Don't tell me what they said about me. Tell me why they were so comfortable telling you** ~ This is a powerful message that everyone should read. How many times have one of your friends said to you "So and so said this about you, and this, and that." I am guessing a lot. Why? Because they enjoy the drama. Most people do. But the real question is: Why was that person so comfortable telling your 'friend' negative things about you. And the answer is because they have sh*t-talked you before. I want you to know that that person is not a true friend. They might think that they are, but they are not. A real friend talks about your shortcomings to you. They do not talk to others negatively about you. Cowards do that. Always be on the lookout for this subtle type of attack and cut them off.

373. **Sometimes you have to go through the darkness to get to the light** ~ I want you to know that it is okay to be lost in life, to be angry at the world and to be angry at yourself. In fact, it's better than okay because there are great advantages to feeling badly. And it doesn't matter if you do not see them right now, just know that deep down inside those dark moments lies the greatest opportunity, the chance to reinvent yourself. It doesn't matter who you were before or what you used to do. Take out a piece of paper and start writing. Write down the person you want to become, the legend you have always wanted to be, and then use and manipulate your anger into providing the motivation to actually become that person.

374. **You can't stop someone who knows where they're going** ~ Most people don't have a direction for where they want to go in their life. For the select few that do know, it's going to be impossible to stop them. When someone is on a mission that is greater than themselves, it's magical to see what happens. If you're working a job or living a life you hate, what do you have to lose? You know what your passion is: It's already inside of you. You have to be the one to let it manifest itself so you can take pride in who you are. Your uniqueness is what sets you apart, use it to your advantage.

375. **In order for you to insult me, I would first have to value your opinion** ~ Lion rule #1: Live life on your own terms. Pave your own path and create a vision that is specific for you. Don't live your life based on other's expectations or opinions. Lions don't care what the sheep think! The only opinions that should matter to you are from people who are doing what you want to do in life. That being said, follow your intuition and go after your vision while not giving a care in the world what the majority might have to say!

376. **When looking back doesn't interest you anymore, you are doing something right** ~ Most people look at the past and let that define their future. They believe that if something didn't work out, they're never going to be successful. Look toward the future. Understand that your past doesn't define you in any way. You have the choice every day to be reborn and go after what you want. Are you going to stop feeling sorry for yourself and quit crying like a little b*tch? We all have had to go through things to become successful. Man up and chase after your dreams.

377. **If you knew me yesterday, you don't know me anymore. I grow daily** ~ The person you were yesterday should never be the same person you are today. Are you constantly growing and evolving? Reading books, watching videos, taking courses, networking, and going to seminars? Don't give me the bullsh*t line that you don't have enough time in your day. You're going to have to be uncomfortable. This means getting out of your normal routine and working from the second you wake up until you go to bed. If you want to be successful, you can't be the same person you were yesterday.

378. **My scars tell my story. They remind me of when life tried to break me, but failed** ~ Whether you know it or not, we all have scars. Scars are not always visible, but internal, and it's those internal scars that hurt us the most. Any time you have failed, had problems, depressions, letdowns, or traumatic experiences, those all cause internal scars. They have all made you into the person you are today, and you can either choose to let those problems control you and cry about them forever or you can embrace your troubles and use them to make you a stronger person. It's all about your perception. Just know that it's during those down moments that define you.

379. **I don't have a New Year's resolution. I have a detailed plan for my life** ~ Over 92% of New Year's resolutions are not kept. And that makes sense, because anyone who waits for a specific date on the calendar to change is misguided because changing your lifestyle, habits, and mindset does not happen on one single day. It happens by making small improvements over a long period of time. This is why you need a detailed plan for your life. Someone with a detailed plan does not rely on the external calendar; rather, they look to the internal. They have their whole life planned out. They set yearly, five-year, and ten-year goals and they take their life seriously because they realize they only have one life to accomplish all they wish to accomplish. So, if you haven't yet, make a detailed plan for your life and structure your lifestyle, habits and priorities around that plan.

380. **Do not waste your time on someone who only fits you around when it fits their needs** ~ There are people who want to use you in every area of your life. They might lie straight your face. Someone keeps you around for business only because it helps them. You only have sex with that guy or girl for pleasure. They believe you when you tell them it's love. The second that person doesn't want you in their life anymore, they'll be gone. Take a hard look at the people you surround yourself with. Do they really like you for you, or is it in their best interest? Once you find these people, you must dismiss them from your life.

381. **Never push a loyal person to the point where they no longer give a f*ck** ~ When you have someone who's been by your side the entire time from the beginning, the worst thing you can do is f*ck that person over. There will come a day when that person no longer wants anything to do with you. You'll let them leave, not thinking much of it. Somewhere down the line, you're going to need that person. When you come calling, they'll leave you in a pit of emptiness, wondering where it all went wrong.

382. **Always find time for the things that make you feel happy to be alive** ~ Life moves fast. We can spend so much time working that we forget to create experiences. The reason we grind is to live a better life. To be able to take a vacation whenever we'd like. You can make copious amounts of money, but you only have a certain amount of time left. If you spend it behind your desk, you're going to miss out. To be wealthy means more than having money—it means to live an adventurous life and have loving relationships. This doesn't mean to neglect the money aspect; make as much as you can. But don't forget other aspects of life.

383. **When you forgive, you heal. When you let go, you grow** ~ You can't hold a grudge against everyone who has wronged you. It takes a lot more energy to hate someone, so don't bother. Forgive them if they have wronged you. They have to live with that, you don't. No matter what you try to do, you can't take back what they've done. Forgive, but never forget. Forgiving allows you to heal your wounds and to move on. This can be in a relationship or starting a business. Always be in control of your emotions and never let them get the best of you.

384. **Choose me or lose me. I'm not a backup plan and I'm definitely not a second choice** ~ People will come into your life and sometimes they might leave. If they leave, there's never a need to reconcile. They made that decision and now you're making a decision on your own. You are never anyone's backup plan. You have to know your own worth and that's a lot more than someone who leaves you. This includes friends and partners. Be around people who appreciate you and make you feel loved. There's no place to hold onto people who no longer wish to be with you. Move on and focus on becoming the best version of yourself.

385. **A wise person knows that there's something to be learned from everything** ~ If you go through life thinking you know it all, you're wrong. Do you understand how long it would take to learn everything in the world? An infinite amount of time. This is why you can use your communication skills to learn from others. You can learn something good and bad from every person you meet. Don't look down upon anyone or act as if you're better than anyone else. You may be skillful in one subject but an idiot in another. Never let your ego get the best of you. Keep yourself grounded as you continue to learn and grow.

386. **Don't just talk about the grind. Be about the grind** ~ Putting in serious work every day is becoming a lost art, and it's being replaced by people who only talk about their dreams and goals but never actually work toward them. Why? Because talking is easy and taking action is hard. Make a pact with yourself today that no more will you be just talking about your grind, instead, you will let your actions speak for themselves. Let others know you by your work ethic and stay quiet during your rise to power and success.

387. **I'm tired of following orders, it's time to build my own empire** ~ There comes a time in every person's life when they are done... Done with blindly taking orders, done with blindly following the status quo, and done living their life by another person's version of a 'successful life.' And if that is what you are feeling like right now, listen up: You were born into this world for a purpose. You were born into this world to find your greatness and to create yourself. No more playing it small and thinking small. Tell yourself the sheep games are over! And from this day forward, you will be a Lion and grow your empire to new heights. No surrender!

388. **When you start seeing your worth, you'll find it hard to stay around people who don't** ~ Don't settle for just any or job or any partner. You deserve so much more. Understand your own worth, what you bring to the table. Hang around people who appreciate the value you have. Over time, you'll realize the people that you need to break away from. It may not be easy, but it has to be done. Never lower yourself or your standards for anyone else. If anything, raise them up to yours. Remember, this is your life, you determine how the story is written.

389. **I put zero weight into anyone's opinion about me, because I know exactly who I am** ~ How many of you get offended by what so-and-so says about you? Or what someone on social media says about you? Well, you shouldn't. You should only care about what your true friends and close family think of you, and even that should be limited. So stop wasting valuable time keeping up to date with what this person or that person is saying about you. You have more important things to do. Let them think whatever the hell they want; it doesn't change who you are or what you stand for. You need to realize that life's losers have nothing better to do than point out faults in others. Let them. They are sheep and Lions do not care about their opinions. Lions are true to themselves and are the world's strongest individuals.

390. **Confuse them with your silence and amaze them with your actions** ~ We all know this type of person: all talk and no results. These people are rampant throughout society. They love to talk about their future plans, but fail to act on those plans to make them more than just plans... and some of them just blame others for their lack of success... Well, I'm here to tell you that Lions do not do this. Lions let their results speak for themselves. Lions speak little but are well known for their results because they are life's action-takers. They don't give a crap about the people's opinion of them because they actually produce results and can accomplish their goals... it's time to stay quiet and it's time to take massive action.

391. **Great men are not born great. They grow great through discipline, honor, and grit** ~ Unless you were born special, you have to earn power, riches and prestige, and you do that through discipline, honor, and most especially with grit. We all know the concepts of discipline and honor, but what is grit? Grit is the ability to be consistent every day doing what you need to do in order to fulfill your dream. Men with grit are uncommon men. Men with grit are life's game-changers, the visionaries, the workaholics, and life's most powerful people. Becoming a person of greatness doesn't happen overnight nor does it have to do with genetics. It has to do solely with your power—your mind, your persona, and your level of grit. Grow into the person you want to be by writing out what you want to be like and going after it every day. It's that simple. Do not pretend it is a hard concept.

392. This is a ruthless world and one must be ruthless to cope with it ~ You are not going to get to the top by being soft. You get to the top by staring down your competitors and enemies and meeting them face to face. If you wanted to gain respect during the Roman Empire, you had to show acts of bravery. You didn't talk behind other people's backs or feel you were deserving even though you didn't do any work. Make a pact to yourself, that in business and with your finances, you are going to be a strong person. Not a timid sheep who lets others trample over them, but a Lion who is clear-cut in their actions and will apologize zero times for getting ahead in life.

393. Build the strength to let go of anything that no longer grows you ~ There will be times in your life when the opportunities or the people you hang around with are no longer needed. These are the people and events that hold you back from living a life of purpose. This includes negative friends and jobs that you aren't satisfied with. Are you constantly learning and improving each day? The world has tons of content that you could be learning from: Podcasts, books, YouTube videos, online courses, blog posts—the options are endless. There is no reason you can't become an expert in your industry if you're willing to put in the time. Take each day as a whole and see it as an opportunity to grow.

394. Never sacrifice 3 things: your family, heart or dignity ~ I'm a big fan of sacrificing for your future... sacrifice your time, energy and sweat for the betterment of your future... but NOT your family, heart or dignity. These three are more important than all the money in the world. Your family should never be tampered with. Spend time with them and provide for them, always. "A man who doesn't spend time with his family can never be a real man"... and that goes without saying, never cheat. Never go against your morals and stay true to who you are and never waver based on the 'opportunity '.

395. **My life, my choices, my mistakes, my lessons. None of your business. ~** To become a master of anything or to become the top in your field, you will need to go through many obstacles, mistakes and setbacks... and anyone who says it's an easy ride knows nothing about the path towards mastery and massive success... While you climb the ladder, especially at the beginning, it will be hard. You will go through ups and downs, laughable failures and huge setbacks. People will judge you and talk about you, but do not worry. This is all a part of the process. No one ever got to the top without haters talking about them. They got there by hearing them but choosing to ignore them. They are losers. This is, not theirs. Never settle in your life, you were meant for Greatness.

396. **Strong people do not put others down. They lift them up. ~** A tell-tale sign of an insecure person is if that person is always putting other people down... a person who puts others down routinely is a very damaged person. Don't take what they are saying to heart, because they are totally misguided and their opinion means nothing... on the other hand, the strong man supports, inspires and motivates his fellow man. He doesn't put people down... that wouldn't make him feel good nor would he get any pleasure from it. The strong man is secure with himself and what he does. Action step: proactively stop yourself from putting anyone down and proactively stop yourself from surrounding yourself with those people that do.

397. **Never let someone who has done nothing tell you how to do anything. ~** Only listen to people who have done what you are trying to do. The world is full of preachers, but not action takers. Talk is the cheapest commodity while action requires guts and discipline. Which makes this world a lot easier for people willing to put in the work. If you are an action taker, your next step is to find mentors, if not in person, through books. Stop listening to your family or friends when it comes to financial decisions if they are not where you want to be. I paid for a mentor when I was 19 years old and 6 months later, with limited capital, I was making 6 figures a year. Of course, that required relentless action, but I never would have done it that quickly without the help of a mentor. Start taking action & follow the 'Greats', not life's many preachers.

398. **Train your mind to be calm in every type of situation ~** In life, have the attitude of a warrior. Through every situation, circumstance and day to day struggle, remain calm. A warrior has complete control over his mind - no matter the chaos that ruptures around him, inside, he is untethered. The art of being calm amidst chaos is hard, which is why you must train your mind daily. Action step: practice 5 minutes of quiet meditation every day and then move on to 10 minutes. Add 5 minutes every week until you can do an hour straight... and don't mind other people's judgements. They are not warriors and their opinions are of zero value.

399. **5:00 A.M is the hour when legends are either waking up or going to bed. ~** Legends are different. Legends are the opposite of average... they got to the top by doing things differently. They work while others sleep. Whether that's by waking up extremely early or staying up extremely late. They are grinding alone, building their future. They do things their own way and do not subscribe to the average person's mindset. Action step: if you are a natural early bird, start waking up before 5. If you are a natural night owl, work throughout the night... these are how legends are made, grinding, while everyone is asleep.

400. **Do your future self a favor and work hard now. ~** So many of us Lions have goals and visions for the future. Yet, many of us have a hard time getting here... and that is because you are living too much in the future and not enough in the present. It's time to focus on the present and the present only. Your future is a result of what you do day to day... so focus day to day! Every night write down your top 5 objectives for the next day, and when you wake up, do the most important thing first. No retreats. No surrender. Go all in, every single day... and before you know it, you'll be living your vision.

Made in the USA
San Bernardino, CA
20 May 2017

America Through Time is an imprint of Fonthill Media LLC

Fonthill Media LLC
www.fonthillmedia.com
office@fonthillmedia.com

First published 2015

ISBN 978-1-63500-025-2

Typeset in Mrs Eaves XL Serif Narrow
Printed and bound in England

Connect with us:
www.twitter.com/usathroughtime
www.facebook.com/AmericaThroughTime